Comedia Series ● No – 17

Weymouth College
Learning for Life

Lit
Tel:

NINETEEN EIGHTY-FOUR IN 1984

AUTONOMY, CONTROL AND COMMUNICATION

Edited by Paul Chilton and Crispin Aubrey

Comedia Publishing Group
9 Poland Street, London W1V 3D
In association with Maryon Boyar

Comedia Publishing Group was set up to investigate and monitor the media in Britain and abroad. The aim of the project is to provide basic information, investigate problem areas, and to share the experiences of those working in the field, while encouraging debate about the future development of the media. The opinions expressed in the books in the Comedia series are those of the authors, and do not necessarily reflect the views of Comedia. For a list of other Comedia titles see page 121.

First published in 1983 by Comedia Publishing Group
9 Poland Street, London W1 3DG.

First published 1983
Reprinted 1984

ISBN 0 906 890 43 8 (paperback)
ISBN 0 906 890 42 X (hardback

Cover Design by Will Hill
Visuals by Bill Evans

Typeset by Photosetting & Secretarial Services Ltd.
Station Approach, Yeovil, Somerset. Tel: Yeovil 23684

Printed in Great Britain by
Unwin Brothers Ltd., The Gresham Press, Old Woking, Surrey

Trade Distribution by
Marion Boyars, 18 Brewer Street, London W1

Distributed in United States of America by
Marion Boyars Publishers Inc., The Scribner Book Companies

Contents

Introduction   1

INTERPRETATIONS

1. The Making of 1984. *Crispin Aubrey*   7

2. Reclaiming Orwell. *David Widgery*   15

3. Desire is Thoughtcrime. *Jenny Taylor*   24

COMMUNICATIONS

4. Newspeak: It's The Real Thing. *Paul Chilton*   33

5. The Tyranny of Language. *Florence Lewis*
   and *Peter Moss*   45

TECHNOLOGIES

6. Taming the Universal Machine. *Christopher Roper*   58

7. The Robots' Return? *Mike Cooley* and *Mike Johnson*   71

8. Information as Power. *Paul Lashmar*   79

ENVIRONMENT

9. Big Brother Drives a Bulldozer. *Colin Ward*   89

10. Hard Machines, Soft Messages. *Philip Corrigan*   98

11. The Conscription of History. *Patrick Wright*   105

Biographies   115

Notes   116

Paul Chilton
Introduction

There are a lot of things you can do with a novel. One is to ignore it, especially if it is awkward and won't fit unequivocally into some literary or ideological slot. George Orwell's *Nineteen Eighty-Four* was not ignored in 1949 when it was first published, and in 1984 still cannot be easily avoided, even if you haven't read it. For those of Orwell's generation, it could not be ignored, because the novel bore (it still does) the marks of the bitter political disputes and in-fighting of the thirties and forties. Those, who, like the majority of the contributors to the present book, were children when the novel was written, could not avoid it because it was taught in school by teachers of literature. And the present generation, and anyone else who may not have read it, cannot avoid it because its key words have entered daily speech. After 1066, 1984 is perhaps the best known date in English history. In fact, '1984' is less a date than a symbol. Vague and ambivalent (as symbols are), it stands for a cluster of political fears. But it also implies *resistance* – in spite of, or perhaps because of the ultimate submission of Winston Smith to Big Brother in the story of *Nineteen Eighty-Four*.

No sooner had *Nineteen Eighty-Four* been written, than it was instantly claimed for the Right. Fredric Warburg, Orwell's publisher, said: '*1984* is ... worth a cool million votes to the Conservative Party; it is imaginable that it might have a preface by Winston Churchill after whom its hero is named.' While some reviewers saw it as an attack neither on Communism nor Socialism, but as an attack on all forms of totalitarian tendency, there were many (including Communists) who saw it as, in Isaac Deutscher's words, 'a sort of ideological superweapon in the cold war'. But in recent years key ideas and clichés from *Nineteen Eighty-Four* have been used by both sides in the nuclear arms debate. Alun Chalfont accuses CND of 'newspeak' (*Encounter Pamphlet* 13); CND accuses its opponents of 'nukespeak'. In the 1983 general election a caller to a radio phone-in programme asked the Defence Minister whether acceptance of American cruise missiles and military bases did not make Great Britain look like Airstrip One – Orwell's name for Great Britain in the novel. The division of the world into rival superpowers is probably the closest and most significant point of resemblance between *Nineteen Eighty-Four* and 1984, and it is an aspect of the novel that Orwell himself stressed particularly in a communiqué issued (ironically perhaps) through Warburg himself: 'Specifically the danger lies in the structure imposed on Socialist and on Liberal capitalist communities by the necessity to prepare for total war with the U.S.S.R. and the new weapons, of which of course the atomic bomb is the most powerful ...'.[1] The Minister's reply to the comparison with *Nineteen Eighty-Four* was interesting. As the real 1984 approached, it was necessary for the Conservatives to allay fears that the Orwellian 1984 would arrive with *their* return to office! Had they not said in a 1979 election poster: Where will you be in 1984 if *Labour* wins? So the Minister said: 'I've read *Nineteen Eighty-Four* and we'd all agree, I think, that relatively few of Orwell's forecasts have come true'. ('Election Call', Radio 4, 31 May, 1983). He did not say whether he included doublethink among the failed forecasts.

There is no doubt then that the novel not only has relevance, but that in addition it actually plays some kind of role in the processes of political discourse – a rare achievement for a work of literature. But it is an ambiguous novel, and given the range of social forms it alluded to – bolshevism, capitalism, nazism, catholicism, ancient slave societies, Platonic utopias[2] – it wasn't surprising that readers paid their money and took their pick. William Empson had warned Orwell of such things after *Animal Farm*. It is plain from Orwell's own statements that it was not his intention to criticise socialism in general – but the text does allow readers to deduce different intentions.

It is of course possible to lift *Nineteen Eighty-Four* out of the arena of political discourse, indeed out of history, altogether. One way of doing this is to insist, as some reviewers did from the outset, that the novel is not so much (or not at all) about state oppression, but about private obsession, depression, neurosis. (This technique for 'explaining' crisis in modern societies is discussed further by Phil Corrigan, in chapter 10). It was and is all too easy to turn the novel into psychopathology, by linking it with Orwell's supposed experience of an authoritarian prep school (described in his essay 'Such, Such Were the Joys') by emphasizing his undoubted class-ridden sense of guilt, or by pointing to the sado-masochism of the novel and even to an oedipal relationship between Winston and his torturer-saviour, O'Brien. The specific political messages can equally be suppressed by making it out to be a general fantasy of human fears or an allegorical portrayal of the human condition. More recent trends in literary criticism (some of those calling themselves 'structuralist', 'post-structuralist' and 'deconstructionist') would end up seeing the book as a self-referring hall of mirrors cut off from historical processes.

Nothing could be further from the drift of the present collection of essays. In a sense they all return to the attitude towards the novel that many readers adopted in 1948. They let *Nineteen Eighty-Four* refer to 1984, that is, to their own way of interpreting 1984. Of course, there are several ways in which it *could* refer to now, and many ways in which today's world can be interpreted. Most people (including Mr Heseltine) have read the novel as prediction or forecast. The advantage of that for them is that predictions are either true or false: old Orwell simply got it wrong and we can forget about him. Another possibility is – or perhaps was – to read it as a sort of warning: if you don't do x, then y will follow. Then you can say that since we are clearly not literally in Orwell's *Nineteen Eighty-Four*, the warning has been duly heeded: no more need to worry. A rather different possibility is to see the novel as some sort of political theorising concerning the nature of the totalitarian state – a kind of thought-experiment to see what happens when total political control is postulated. The important problems that arise when this stance is taken have often been pointed out by critics. Is it really possible for naked power to sustain itself without some legitimating ideology, as it seems to in the novel? Are the 'proles' *really* like Orwell's portrayal of them, and what lies behind the novel's statement that it is in them that all hope lies?

All these ways of using the novel are to some degree illuminating, all show up some weaknesses in the novel. The contributors to the present book certainly make use of these approaches, but what they do in addition is to use *Nineteen Eighty-Four* as a way of looking *metaphorically* at the other 1984. Metaphor is a way of looking at things that heightens some similarities and neglects others. Orwell himself spoke of his novel as a kind of satire, a kind of parody: it was a way of looking at the way things *could* (not necessarily *would*, as he stressed) turn out, when you looked at the world in 1948. 'He did possess a terrible intensity of vision, capable of picking out a single hidden truth and then magnifying it.' This was Orwell on Swift in his essay 'Politics vs. Literature', but it is a reasonable way of thinking about Orwell's novel too. To read *Nineteen Eighty-Four* this year is to sensitise yourself to those aspects of 1984 that *did* turn out just like, more like, or less like the novel suggests, and also to sensitise yourself to those things that *could* have turned out that way but didn't.

The first section of the book, 'Interpretations', deals in more detail with some of the themes just discussed. Crispin Aubrey sets the novel in its historical context, clarifies the nature of Orwell's intentions, and examines the reception of the book. David Widgery and Jenny Taylor both discuss the highjacking of the book by the Right, while indicating the ways in which it lent itself to appropriation. Both see it as a challenge to radical interpretation. Widgery shows how *Nineteen Eighty-Four* can be reclaimed by the anti-Stalinist Left, but points out its inadequacies. Taylor develops the kind of critique Orwell would never have imagined, and probably would not have understood, to show up internal contradictions in his representation of women, the family and sexuality, which are not only revealing for the novel but also for 1984. It is clear that the meaning of *Nineteen Eighty-Four* – just as the meaning of 1984 – will vary, depending on when you read it (1948 is not 1984), and who you are and what are your ideological assumptions.

In the remaining sections of the book, particular aspects of the social and political fabric are looked at through the novel. In 1948 Orwell had no way of foreseeing the technological developments of the next forty years. He seemed to be grasping the quantum leap implied by the advent of atomic bombs; but computers and information technology were only crudely and dimly foreshadowed in the novel. He remained in the age of the machine, and used the machine metaphorically. The state becomes a machine, so does propaganda and ideology. The most creative aspects of human consciousness he sees as in the process of mechanisation. It is easy to think that electronic processing and transmission of information would have been viewed in a similar way by Orwell. It is quite common for people in 1984 to extend the Orwellian nightmare to express fears of a wired-up world dominated by impersonal electronic devices. Christopher Roper questions the justification of such fears, points out in detail the potential benefits, arguing that the Left has failed to come to terms with the revolutionary implications of the rapid change in the processing of information. Mike Cooley and Mike Johnson are less confident that technology can be an independent cause of social progress. It is clear from their work, both here and elsewhere, that technologies can be used for control not just of work but of workers, and that, as Orwell imagined, though not in the precise way he imagined, technology can lead to the dehumanisation of all types of work, including those that are usually thought of as being the most creative and most basically human. The potential of modern electronic technology not only for good, but also for realising the wildest dreams of Big Brother is discussed by Paul Lashmar. The electronic means are there, if not the scale.

Control in a different, less tangible, but more pervasive sense is discussed in the section on Communication. Orwell's notion of 'newspeak' is an illuminating, if imprecise, means of making oneself conscious of the deceptions – the deliberate deceptions – of language, and its role in the maintaining of structures of power. My own paper is in part an attempt to show how the world of *Nineteen Eighty-Four* transposes to today's world of televised swindling and bamboozling, but also to show how nobody need be taken in in the way Orwell's theory of newspeak seems to imply you can be taken in. Peter Moss and Florence Lewis make sense of *Nineteen Eighty-Four*'s crude methods of censorship and reality control in terms of today's more subtle institutions. They show how selection operates in the press, radio and television, how the new communications technology from video cassettes to satellites results in the control of leisure and of one's perceptions of reality. Their view of newspeak in 1984 focuses on the destruction of private feeling, which they relate to the presence of terror and violence in both politics and entertainment. Against this picture of culture and language, one should not overlook David Widgery's view that some forms of popular culture have in fact become less not more restricted.

Colin Ward, in the section on the Environment, maintains that hope still lies in the proles in the inner city, where official planning has destroyed local communities along with their physical environment – the 'prole quarters' sentimentally and perhaps ambivalently described by Orwell. *Nineteen Eighty-Four* represents the proles as embodying a kind of natural, naïve and almost rustic spirit, and Ward relates this view to the 'urban peasantry' who are unemployed, yet employed, in the underground culture of the underground economy. Widgery, in his opening chapter, sees this aspect of Orwell's view of the working class as a specific weakness in his conception of the social and political process. It is based on nostalgia, as is Winston's love of old books, bric-à-brac and fusty furniture. In 'The Conscription of History' Patrick Wright extends this experience to illuminate the way in which in 1984 the past is recalled and frozen (like the world in Winston's antique glass paper weight) at different strata of society in a specific inner-city locality. Different worlds, different evocations of the past coexist, and above them all, imposed from the top down are other national nostalgias and national myths, which may conflict with those of people whose past is neither white, nor British, nor middle class. Philip Corrigan's chapter, like Widgery's and Taylor's, though in quite different terms, takes on some of the fundamental differences between the model of society implicit in *Nineteen Eighty-Four* and the social forms with which we are now confronted. In general Orwell's novel fails to capture the development of consumer capitalism after the Second World War: the abundance, variety, brightness, sexual freedom contrast with *Nineteen Eighty-Four*'s drab, dingy, puritanical environment. This is not to say that repression, suffering and misery do not occur – they do, but they are conditioned by the 'soft messages' of 'choice' and 'freedom', another aspect of newspeak, which argues that those who do not enjoy them are failures in need of treatment. *Nineteen Eighty-Four* is not 1984 in any direct or literal sense. It is very odd, if you think about it, that anyone should ever think that a novel ever *could* accomplish such a feat, let alone that it should.

BILL EVANS

Chapter 1

Crispin Aubrey
The Making of 1984

Alongside *Animal Farm*, *Nineteen Eighty-Four* was George Orwell's most commercially successful novel. Since its first publication in 1949, the various editions have run to over 15 million copies around the world. In Britain, the Penguin paperback (first published in 1954) has contributed over three million copies, and is still being turned out at the rate of 175,000 a year – as many as an above average current best-seller. Translations have taken the story of Winston Smith's struggle against Big Brother into 23 languages apart from English. There have been film versions for both the cinema and TV, as well as radio adaptations; and the title itself has become a by-word for the oppressive state apparatus of control, surveillance and suppression – though usually more synonymous with the leather glove cupped round the mouth than the full frontal fist.

Despite Orwell's denials that he was concerned with prediction, he has also proved comparatively successful as a seer. Thirty-five years later, helicopters *do* hover over city centre rooftops watching the human activity below, and surveillance by the state *has* reached the point where it is at least possible to gain the sort of personal information the telescreen could spy, even if not by the same direct method. On the details, the metrication of liquids (though not quite yet in pubs), the weekly public Lotteries (Premium Bonds or the Sun/Star bingo) and the potentially stupefying effect of pop music lyrics, are all close enough to the truth. The continuous war as desensitised spectacle on the film/TV screen – 'Then there was a wonderful shot of a child's arm going up up up right up into the air a helicopter with a camera in its nose must have followed it up' – has also accurately been compared to the nightly newsreels of Vietnam (or Northern Ireland?). And at a global political level, the division of the world into superpower blocs, especially the portrayal of the Third World as 'a bottomless reserve of cheap labour', has proved perceptively accurate.

After that, the conjecture begins. Like many authors, Orwell committed very little to print about his motivation or starting point on the road to *Nineteen Eighty-Four*. In those private letters which *have* been published, he invariably talks obscurely about the project, almost as though he were unwilling to reveal even the smallest detail of a valuable commercial secret. And certainly there is scarcely enough in his other writing to indicate adequately why a man apparently committed to socialism should write a book which, following on the heels of the satirical *Animal Farm*, is both pessimistic in the extreme and views the future for revolutionary change in a way which has been repeatedly interpreted as virulently *anti*-socialist.

Orwell said himself that he first had the idea for *Nineteen Eighty-Four* during 1943, although it wasn't until three years later, in the aftermath of the Second World War, that he started the writing proper. By that time, at the age of 42, he was just beginning to enjoy the financial and emotional security of literary success, notably with the publication at the end of the War of *Animal Farm*. He could also look back on an extremely varied writing output, from his Jack London-style excursions into the world of down-and-outs (in Paris and London) through his classic descriptions of Northern working class life (in *The Road to Wigan Pier*) to his graphic account of fighting on the Republican side in the Spanish Civil War (*Homage to Catalonia*). There was also a clutch of novels about contemporary British life written with an inimitably dry but sympathetic humour, as well as his position as a noted literary critic, reviewer and political essayist on the Left. Among other publications, he was a regular contributor to *Tribune*, a then much more influential magazine which Orwell described as 'the one paper in England which had neither supported the Government uncritically, nor opposed the war, nor swallowed the Russian myth.'

At the same time as fame and security, however, came illness. Orwell had been slowly succumbing to a tuberculosis which he had known to exist for some time, and spent a considerable part of his last few years in and out of hospitals and sanitoria. When not studying the end of a hospital bed, he retired to a remote farmhouse on the Scottish island of Jura, where much of *Nineteen Eighty-Four* was in fact written. Never one for great creature comforts, these were still extremely spartan conditions for a sick man to work in. Suffering from high temperatures whenever he exerted himself, his lungs inflamed, he found it difficult even to type. The final version of the novel was reportedly typed partly in bed, partly sitting on a chair, and in a room heated by a faulty paraffin stove whose atmosphere Orwell further polluted with the smoke of his own work-enhanced consumption of cigarettes.

'The execution would have been better if I had not written it under the influence of TB,' he told his publisher Fredric Warburg in a letter written during October, 1948. 'I ballsed it up rather, partly owing to being so ill while I was writing ...' he told fellow author Julian Symons in another letter a few months' later. By the time the book was actually published, in the summer of 1949, Orwell was back in hospital again – and at the beginning of a downhill path from which he never recovered.

Some critics have used the clearly desperate state of Orwell's health as an explanation for the apparently overwhelming pessimism of *Nineteen Eighty-Four*, suggesting the novel to be almost the morbid ravings of a dying man. But however much his encroaching tuberculosis may have encouraged the tone, or made the result stylistically flawed in parts, it's clearly not an incoherent or ill-considered book. Pointing out that Orwell was already planning a new novel before *Nineteen Eighty-Four* was even completed, biographer Bernard Crick asserts that this was 'no last testament: it was simply the last major work he wrote before he happened to die.'

One other factor is important in assessing the effect of Orwell's illness on the novel. That is the few notes which do exist of the ideas he jotted down for the outline of the book. These were left by Orwell in University College Hospital, and include an accurate running sequence of the plot as it turned out, as well as brief references to Newspeak, the Party and its slogans, the Two Minutes Hate and so on (the entire document is reprinted in Bernard Crick's *George Orwell: A Life*, 1980). These have been dated as being written no later than the beginning of 1944, making it clear that the book was carefully conceived well before Orwell's later chronic decline in health.

This outline also militates against another theory for the genesis of *Nineteen Eighty-Four*. This is that Orwell effectively lifted the story from E. I. Zamyatin's *We*, another classic anti-Utopian novel originally written in 1923, though subsequently banned in the author's native Soviet Union and then published in Paris. *We* is the saga of two numbered members, D503 and I330, of a future 'total state' run by 'The Benefactor', who fall in love (a crime), become involved in a rebellion and are eventually given the necessary 'treatment' in order to be successfully incorporated back. 'I am interested in that kind of book, and even keep making notes for one myself which may get written sooner or later,' Orwell wrote to an expatriate Soviet professor in 1944 having for the first time been alerted about Zamyatin. But it wasn't until 1946, long after he had written his own futuristic outline, that he finally obtained a copy of *We* (in French) and reviewed it for *Tribune*. In this he sees the target of the book as not so much the Soviet system as 'industrial civilisation' in general (an interesting comparison to *Nineteen Eighty-Four*). 'It is in effect a study of the Machine,' he wrote, 'the genie that man has thoughtlessly let out of its bottle and cannot put back again.' Of course, it could be that he injected details from *We* into his own script, but whatever the similarity Orwell's is indisputably marked out with his own unique style and tone.

Only a few other *direct* indications for the origins of his specific ideas in *Nineteen Eighty-Four* exist in his writings. The 'zones of influence' concept through which the world was divided into Eastasia, Eurasia and Oceania came from a mixture of the 1943 world-dividing conferences in Teheran between Churchill, Stalin and Roosevelt, and James Burnham's *Managerial Revolution*, in which a tripartite division of the world is envisaged, each part ruled by a 'self-elected oligarchy'. For the internal layout of the Ministry of Truth, where his hero works, Orwell is said to have used his own workplace, the BBC; whilst his consistent fascination with the use and abuse of the English language clearly led him into Newspeak. 'The solution I suggest (to the lack of precision in certain areas of English),' he wrote in 1940, 'is to invent new words as deliberately as we would invent new parts for a motor-car engine.'

But if proof were needed that the basic ideas of *Nineteen Eighty-Four* were part of Orwell's developing political attitude, and not the sudden quirk of an ill man, then listen to this from the earlier *Coming up for Air*:

'It isn't the war that matters (muses the anti-hero George Bowling), it's the after-war. The world we're going down into, the kind of hate-world, slogan world. The barbed wire. The rubber truncheons. The secret cells where the electric light burns night and day and the detective watching you while you sleep. And the processions and the posters with enormous faces, and the crowds of a million people all cheering for the Leader till they deafen themselves into thinking that they really worship him, and all the time, underneath, they hate him so that they want to puke. It's all going to happen. Or is it? Some days I know it's impossible, other days I know it's inevitable.'

Even before the book was published, there were disagreements about what it meant. The publicity department of publishers G. Warburg produced a blurb which suggested (to Orwell) that it was a mixture of thriller and love story. Behind the scenes, Fredric Warburg himself also gave a private indication (in an internal memo to the firm) of how many radical intellectuals of the time might view it. Having described it as 'terrifying' and 'pessimism unrelieved', Warburg deduced that Orwell had abandoned socialism as an ideal. 'It is worth a cool million votes to the Conservative Party; it is imaginable that it might have a preface by Winston Churchill after whom its hero is named,' he added dryly.

Nineteen Eighty-Four was an immediate success. Published in both New York and London during June, 1949, it sold over 400,000 copies in the first year, and was quickly surrounded by controversy. Many reviewers treated it as a horrifying warning of how discernable trends in post-war society could develop; others, like V. S. Pritchett, as a satire on the 'moral corruption of absolute power'. It 'goes through the reader like an east wind,' Pritchett wrote in the *New Statesman*, 'cracking the skin, opening the sores; hope has died in Mr. Orwell's wintry mind, and only pain is known.' But a broad thrust of immediate criticism was that the novel was a bitter attack on the Soviet Union and its social system, anti-Communist and even anti-socialist in general. Some American magazines identified Ingsoc directly with the British Labour Party.

A typical example of the invective to which the book was subjected is this, from Marxist historian A. L. Morton:

'The whole account ... is tricked out with a pretence of philosophic discussion, but as an intellectual attack on Marxism it is beneath contempt. What Orwell does with great skill is to play upon the lowest fears and prejudices engendered by bourgeois society in dissolution. His object is not to argue a case but to induce an irrational conviction in the minds of his readers that any attempt to realise socialism must lead to a world of corruption, torture and insecurity. To accomplish this no slander is too gross, no device too filthy: *Nineteen Eighty-Four* is, for this country at least, the last word to date in counter-revolutionary apologetics.'

(*The English Utopia*, 1952)

Pravda described it (in 1950) as 'slobbering with poisonous spittle ... he imputes every evil to the people ... It is clear that Orwell's filthy book is in the spirit of such a vital organ of American propaganda as the *Reader's Digest* which published this work.'

Orwell is said to have been considerably upset by what he saw as confusion of his idea and motive. He even issued a statement through his publishers in which he denied the book as prediction and painted a picture of both socialist *and* capitalist countries on the fragile brink – especially with the recent advent of the atomic bomb – of a new potential fascism. 'If there is a failure of nerve and the Labour Party breaks down in its attempt to deal with the hard problems with which it will be faced,' he wrote, 'tougher types than the present Labour leaders will inevitably take over, drawn probably from the ranks of the Left, but not sharing the Liberal aspirations of those now in power.' The book was set in Britain, he added (in a later comment to an American trade union wanting clarification), 'in order to emphasize that the English-speaking races are not innately better than anyone else and that totalitarianism, *if not fought against*, could triumph anywhere.'

This reaction did not stop the continuing interpretation of the book as the product of a man of evidently middle class background who had toyed with socialism, found it wanting and eventually decided to expose its festering scabs. In 1955, Isaac Deutscher made a lengthy and influential assault on the novel as 'a sort of ideological superweapon in the Cold War. As in no other book or document, the convulsive fear of Communism, which has swept the West since the end of the Second World War, has been reflected and focussed in *Nineteen Eighty-Four*.' Whatever Orwell's intention, it came over as a symbol of disillusionment with all shades of socialism and a 'cry from the abyss of despair'.

'The shriek, amplified by all the "mass media" of our time, has frightened millions of people,' Deutscher wrote. 'But it has not helped them to see more clearly the issues with which the world is grappling; it has not advanced their understanding. It has only increased and intensified the waves of panic and hate that run through the world and obfuscate innocent minds. *Nineteen Eighty-Four* has taught millions to look at the conflict between East and West in terms of black and white, and it has shown them a monster bogy and a monster scapegoat for all the ills that plague mankind.'

(*Heretics and Renegades*, 1955)

In more recent years, as the immediate political context of its publication has faded, the book has occupied more neutral ideological territory. Unlike with *Animal Farm*, an allegory, readers (and thousands of school students who now read the earlier book as great English literature) are not forced or encouraged to look for literal interpretations or translations. This has almost certainly led to *Animal Farm* often continuing to be read solely as an anti-Communist tract. But it isn't essential to *Nineteen Eighty-Four* to understand that Goldstein is a Trotsky figure against the Stalinist centre of the Party. As a result, the image of Big Brother is now used to conjure up any overweening, bureaucratic use of power, whether by Right or Left. In fact if anything, the Orwellian nightmare is most often employed by the *Left* to encompass the apparatus of control that lies behind the liberal facade of Western democracies. The wheel has come full circle.

How then did George Orwell come to write a book which could be taken so baldly as anti-Communist propaganda? A first point to make is that Orwell was undoubtedly a committed socialist until his death. 'There is really no mystery about the general character of his politics,' as Bernard Crick puts it. 'From 1936 onwards he was first a follower of the Independent Labour Party and then a *Tribune* socialist; that is, he took his stand among those who were to the Left or on the left of the Labour Party: fiercely egalitarian, libertarian and democratic, but by Continental comparisons, surprisingly untheoretical, a congregation of secular evangelicals.' Much of his writing, essays and reviews, was concerned with a critical but sympathetic approach to Left thinking and issues of the day, and to graphically portraying the class system and social inequalities which existed at a time of equally massive unemployment as now. And when he does that, in books like *The Road to Wigan Pier* or an essay about hanging, he portrays another element of his personality – his very English concern for human dignity, fair play, the underdog, combined with a libertarian anti-authoritarianism. A few weeks before his death he is said to have complained that it was totally wrong under a Labour government for such signs of conspicuous wealth as the Rolls Royce to be allowed on the streets.

Orwell's socialism was therefore neither born out of trade union struggles nor the intellectual study of Marxist theories. Encouraged by such personal experiences as his five years in Burma as an officer in the Indian Imperial Police, he had learned to dislike autocratic rule of all types. But he did not look forward to the overthrow of the present system by a violent revolution, rather by convincing people that this was the correct road to take. His unorthodox, libertarian position should appeal in fact to many on the current British left concerned for a broader, more humanitarian socialism. He wrote articles and protested strongly, for example, when the anarchist paper *Freedom* (then titled *War Commentary*) was first raided by the Special Branch and then later prosecuted for 'undermining the affections of His Majesty's Forces'. Three of the editors were sent to prison, an issue which received little attention, Orwell noted, from the then Communist-leaning National Council for Civil Liberties. 'Every line of serious work that I have written since 1936 has been written, directly or indirectly, *against* totalitarianism and *for* democratic Socialism, as I understand it,' he wrote just before the War.

Into that political summary, however, must be put other elements from his experience which set him firmly against both Fascism and Communism. Not only did he live through the period of Hitler and Stalin, but he could not accept the way in which his socialist friends defended the Soviet Union simply because it was the country of the

Bolshevik revolution. In Spain, he saw at first hand on the battlefront both the struggle against Fascism and the way in which, as he saw it, the Communist Party had suppressed the genuine revolution in Catalonia. Taking a strong anti-Communist position on such issues in the period before the Second World War, as he did, was already to be stepping out of line.

In the immediate post-war period, he also saw the first major reforming Labour government of Clement Attlee failing to live up to his expectations. Rationing continued, war damage remained unrepaired, poverty was apparently as endemic as it appears in *Nineteen Eighty-Four*. 'Both Orwell and I expected something more spectacular than Attlee's England of the Beveridge Plan and the Welfare State which followed on the sweeping victory of 1945,' his contemporary, Stephen Spender, wrote in 1978. 'As a material and spiritual phenomenon, this was aptly symbolised by the Festival of Britain on the South Bank of the Thames, with its look of cut-rate cheerfulness cast in concrete and beflagged. Probably the soldiers who attended Army Education courses, and the Civil Defence workers who went to our discussion groups (I think that in *Nineteen Eighty-Four* somewhere Orwell refers to the "solemn farce of a discussion group") were contented with this symbol. But Orwell wanted the symbolism of the Welfare State to be that of manifest revolution.'

Whatever Orwell's ideals at that time, in the novel itself there is an almost total lack of any optimism. This is perhaps what many people find most difficult to take. There is no way out, the labyrinth eventually closes in and engulfs any ray of hope for a different society or even individual expression ... But perhaps we are expecting too much. It is, after all, a *novel* and not a philosophical tract or a political analysis. Orwell took his vision of the future to an extreme because he thought in that way to connect, to make people sit up and think – if not to have nightmare dreams. He evidently succeeded. And to those like myself who find Orwell's mid-summer clarity of style a source of constant pleasure, the achievement is also that he managed to capture the atmosphere of a total state with such sparse descriptive details, with such apparent absence of colouring in. But then it *is* a warning, not a futuristic prophecy, and if *Nineteen Eighty-Four* is set in the context of the writer's entire output, it is not a warning which should upset socialists. In the real 1984, it should remain a spur to action to ensure that nothing like it ever happens.

Chapter 2

David Widgery
Reclaiming Orwell

Orwell remains contested, and *Nineteen Eighty-Four* has to be fought over with particular intensity. It is one of the very few novels that has become a code word capable of evoking pungent political reaction from people who haven't even read it. Readers recall it with a photographic intensity: the rat in Room 101, the public execution, Julia shedding her blouse. But above all the book has been stamped for us with the intense anti-Communism of the Cold War. People of my age – children of '45 and survivors of '68 – all seem to have encountered it taught in classrooms of the Tory Fifties as a combined indictment of the shortages and shoddyness of the first post-war Labour government and of the savagery, secret surveillance and organised dishonesty of some amalgamated hybrid of the Soviet Union in the 1930s with post-war North Korea. Orwell's political ingredients are obviously drawn from wider political source material: the main model is the Soviet Union down to the constantly revised Five Year Plans, the Trotsky-Goldstein figure and the Thought Police – clearly shaped by his first hand experience of the GPU agents' operations against the Spanish Left during the Civil War. But the Youth League's enthusiasm for grassing their parents is specific to Nazi Germany, and the Ministry of Truth is always said to be modelled on the wartime BBC.

It is, of course, also widely known that the politics of the creator of *Nineteen Eighty-Four* were those of an anti-imperialist socialist who, almost uniquely, moved sharply to the Left during the 1930s. But despite his somewhat disingenuous protests, the book has overwhelmingly been utilised as an anti-socialist tract – not merely satirising Stalinist Russia but asserting that a planned economy must mean the end of human freedom. As Charles Murray noted in a recent affectionate appraisal in the *New Musical Express* (Orwell is one of the few socialists popular amongst contemporary rock followers): 'I would not be surprised if – even at this moment – someone is not waving the book at someone else with the baleful cry of "Mark my words, this is what things will be like if your precious Tony Benn got his way".'

For someone like myself, descendant of that tiny anti-Stalinist revolutionary Left tradition with which Orwell had an intimate but uneasy relationship, his last book presents a particular challenge. Orwell stands as one of the very few English men of letters who was, for some of his life, a practising revolutionary socialist. William Morris is the only obvious comparison, and like Orwell his prose work is of uneven value, his political activity unsuccessful and often bogged down in sectarian disputing. It was Orwell who inadvertently coined the motto of the May Events: 'If the problems of western capitalism are to be solved it will have to be through a third alternative, a movement which is genuinely revolutionary, i.e. willing to make drastic changes and use violence if necessary but which does not lose touch, as Communism and Fascism have done, with the essential values of democracy'.

So even if that man's masterpiece is an utterly pessimistic tract which not only savages Stalin's distortions of socialism but projects hatred and cruelty over the very notion of political change, his politics still need to be reviewed and possibly rejected. One has always considered a measure of Orwell's integrity both his identification with the revolutionary wing of the Spanish Republic and his belief that there was no hope for the British Left until it decisively rejected the mythology of Stalinism, all the more so when the intellectuals of the Communist and Labour Left and Centres had swallowed the Moscow line in its entirety and had only really begun to show any enthusiasm for the Soviet Union when it became totalitarian. But if '1984' is really a poisoned chalice then my pro-Soviet friends are perhaps right to denounce him with such special loathing as 'objectively anti-socialist' and just another Koestler-clone who would, had he lived, be writing scripts for Mrs T.

But I think not. On re-reading *Nineteen Eighty-Four* it stands up as an anti-utopian prophesy still coming true, and as satire as harsh to a Free World that isn't free as to a Communist Bloc that isn't Communist. Isn't Britain in fact Airstrip One and haven't we just established a Floating Fortress down by the icecap? Is not Newspeak now at least as good a description of the diplomatic jargon of the Reagan/Thatcher/Kohl axis as of the editorial prose of *Pravda*? Is not Orwell's imagined scene where a cinema audience greets with delight a militaristic variant on Pathé News ominously echoed by the orchestrated jubilation over the torpedoing of the Belgrano?

A large part of the book needs to be reclaimed by the non-Stalinist Left and rescued from the CIA publishing fronts, Radio Free Europe, the Cold War illiberals, Ye Olde New Right and probably from the techy, TB wrapt, exhausted, Orwell himself. It undoubtedly carries the stigmata of political pessimism and personal despair. Its characterisation is negligent, the sub-themes of Goldstein's Testament and the Glossary of Newspeak are awkwardly tacked on, and its emotional structures are, even by Orwell's acerbic standards, unbalanced. It compares unfavourably with less eminent dystopias: Wells has a better sense of the mechanical bustle of the modern world; Huxley was more skilled at anticipating the biochemical, pharmaceutical and genetic trends which have proved so significant; and the incomparable Zamyatin has the immense advantage of writing a utopian experiment within a utopian experiment. But Orwell's dying vision has a remarkable political clarity even if that penetrating gaze ends by ignoring the people, the Plebs, who ought to be the major protagonists.

Take first Orwell's division of the globe into superpower blocs which militarise and bankrupt their own citizens but attain a kind of ghastly economic and social stability from this state of perpetual war. This isn't just an incidental backdrop to Winston Smith's rebellion. When publisher Fredric Warburg's blurb writer wanted to advertise the book as some sort of sex thriller, Orwell refused, insisting that his novel 'is really meant to discuss the implications of dividing the world into "Zones of Influence" ... and in addition to indicate by parodying them intellectual implications of totalitarianism'. From our political vantage point, the Yalta carve-up and the ensuing division of the globe are facts of life. But at the time relatively few people foresaw the new world role American imperialism had won as the prize for rescuing its European imperial seniors – or what Orwell himself called 'the dreary world that the American millionaires and their British hangers on intend to impose on us'. Those who did tended to be members of a Communist Party which had been so slavishly uncritical of the Soviet Union that they were effectively disqualified from credible analysis. Even the Trotskyists were wildly confused, predicting variously immediate crash and collapse in Europe, a workers uprising against the Soviet quislings in the buffer states, or armed socialist insurrections in France, Greece and Northern Italy.

Very few analysts discerned that Western capitalism was entering the most prodigious and prolonged boom in its history and that the permanent arms economy (and later permanent space economy) would play a critical stabilising role. Or that the Soviet Union would complete its transformation from its Bolshevik origins into a new species of state capitalism with a distinct, conservative and none-too-efficient ruling class whose first concern was not fanning the flames of world proletarian insurrection but keeping its own and its empire's workers down. Orwell's sketches are therefore the literary equivalents of the pioneering post-Trotsky, anti-Stalinist unorthodox Marxists of the period like T. N. Vance, T. Cliff and C. L. R. James. And while the early days of the Cold War were conducted in a kind of icy peace, we have grown up to find the two surprisingly symmetrical superpowers (ostensible allies in the last World War) escalate, as mirror images, their shadow wars of arms and ideology which block out independent development elsewhere and press closer and closer to real war.

That celebrated scourge of Orwell, Edward Thompson, has outlined 'a process which has been going on now for more than thirty years, by which the hawks of the West and East have kept on strengthening and feeding each other. Every upward movement in arms on one side meets with an upward movement on the other, and this is not only true of arms but ideological hostilities. When President Reagan rants on about the Soviet Union being an "evil empire", he is actually helping it in that direction since the Soviet rulers respond by tightening up their security system and putting their military preparation into repair.' Is this not precisely, if one includes the post-Mao realignments of China, the oppressive alignment of the superstates of Oceania, Eurasia and Eastasia that Orwell envisaged, where 'the enemy of the moment is always represented as absolutely evil and it followed that any past or future agreement with him was impossible'?

There is within Orwell's forecast a misprediction of the ingredients. His superpowers are more often at open war than ours appear to be (though there have been about 300 wars since 1945 and the major power blocs have been present in most of them, if not as combatants then as armourers, sponsors, intriguers, advisers and provokers). But the scale and power of the weaponry in the real world far outstrips Orwell's worst imaginings. The wars of *Nineteen Eighty-Four* are Exchange and Mart stuff compared with the satellites, rockets, artillery, submarines, toxins, poisons, herbicides, missiles, torpedos and depth charges now in existence. There are currently 18 million full time soldiers in the world, 60,000 combat aircraft and countless aircraft carriers, warships and submarines. One million dollars are spent on arms every minute of the day and night. So Winston Smith's account of a typical film show in which 'the helicopter planted a 20 kilo bomb in among them and the boat went all to matchwood' is not so much horrifying as appallingly modest.

It is not sufficient to note the barbarity of the 1984 permanent war economy as just another aspect of an evil society wired up for continuous surveillance, subjected to continual official dishonesty and short on chocolate. The war economy is the motor of the whole social system and both the cause and the justification for the constant spying and shortages. It is uncannily like Kidron's and Smith's summary of the present day effects of the international military order in *The War Atlas* (Pluto Press, 1983), itself almost a diagram of the real 1984. This doesn't just create dangerous instability between states, they write. 'It is based on conditions within states where power devolves on those who translate its spirit of universal siege into domestic politics. It reinforces the most regressive aspects of each national society. Waste on a collosal scale, centralised power, inaccessible heirachies and overblown bureaucracies are complemented by mutual fear and hostility, the glorification of violence, the disabling of dissent and the curtailing of freedom and human dignity. None of these are new but all owe their contemporary severity to the international military order!'

Orwell was also right to predict how this state of undeclared permanent war would allow the justification of torture to become a way of life not just, as *Guardian* readers like to imagine, for Latin American generals and Siberian work camps but for many of the capitalist democracies. Amnesty International suggests that torture is used widely and routinely in at least 60 modern states. Orwell seems again to have underestimated the scale of political violence. With his deepseated but absurd faith in British 'tolerance', he would have been genuinely shocked to find black and Asian citizens quite regularly stabbed, attacked and treated to arson in the streets of Mayhew and Dickens. And as a consistent defender of the civil liberties of those whose opinions he often abhorred, he would have been incensed by the interrogation techniques used in Northern Ireland, especially after the 1972 introduction of internment. Winston Smith's torture and humiliation is an odd mixture of behaviour therapy, physical and psychological torture, sleep deprivation and, of course, the bloody rat – and has always struck me as implausibly lurid. Having medically examined prisoners who have undergone even short periods of intensive interrogation, I have been shocked at the speed with which modern techniques of disorientation, sense deprivation and apparently quite minor alterations in diet, temperature and daily rhythms can destroy the coherence and confidence of individuals with quite strong belief systems. A prisoner who had survived long terms of conventional solitary confinement told me he found the physical brutality and intimidating prison cell of the old-fashioned 60 days' punishment far easier to endure than the soundless, seamless, impersonality of only one week in a modern maximum security unit.

Perhaps it is this very sophistication which has made it possible for our rulers to make a slow, relatively imperceptible and very 'English' transition into an overcentralised state which is jealous of its secrets, generous with its surveillance, interferes with its local government and trade unions obsessively, and is adept at the art of black propaganda. This is not to succumb to conspiracy theory, to mistake Margaret for Adolf or even to imagine we have an embryo police state in UK '84 (though we do have the odd police city). But it is to be reminded of an old truth, that the British way of doing things, while apparently more polite, is often simply more ruthless. There will always be an England and you will get a nice hot, strong cup of tea after you confess. If they ever do build concentration camps here they will have roses trained over the entrance rather than rampant rodents.

Orwell's quaint machinery of thought control and censorship (the continuously re-written file of *The Times*, the 'memory hole' and Julia's oil can and spanner for the novel writing machine) is in fact *technically* as far away from the modern methods of news management as the rat interrogation is from the noise machines and hoods of Long Kesh. But that system of mental cheating – the professional amoralism operated by the professional newsman – doesn't seem very far away from the leader writers of the yellow press who have perfected hypocrisy as a way of life and denounce the proles for greed, self-interest and fiddled lunch expenses before hurrying off to do exactly the same themselves on ten times the salary. Or the advertising men, those estate agents of the imagination, who can successfully sell anything from a piston ring to a Prime Minister and are then to be heard crying into their cognacs over lunch about the plight of the Labour Party.

Orwell's account of Big Brother's propaganda techniques (ubiquitous loudspeakers, wall to wall two-way TV, Pathé Pictorial war movies and endlessly modified official statements on the progress of production) has also dated badly, and evokes a media somewhere between North Korean TV News and those four-page adverts African military dictatorships take out in the posh papers. Our modern electronic media is more effective because of the inconspicuous way it signals and shapes and nudges its versions of 'accepted values' and 'what is normal' into us. Rather than reading our thoughts, it sells us its products (of which politics is only one). We weren't told to vote for Big Sister and how to hate Michael Foot in the recent tele-carnival which passed for an election, but that was the message. Potential choices of the most serious nature were montaged into party political table tennis matches with the government having all the best camera angles, art direction and matching make-up. 'Issues' were manufactured, 'Opinion' polled in yes/no choices which contained their own conclusions, and the very agenda of what is political was forged before our eyes. The process of continuous alteration of all significant documentation is not required when folk have been made so forgetful by the torrent of misinformation, adverts and light entertainment which become indistinguishable, effortless and instantly forgotten. And lying at the centre of the lying message is a new cruelty which is chillingly Orwellian – from the Blunt-hunt to the vile hounding of Peter Tatchell.

But for all the perception there is also present in *Nineteen Eighty-Four* a terrible cynicism, an almost deliberate extinguishing of political hope which verges on masochism. I think it is very likely that these emotions were linked to the notoriously depressing side effects of pulmonary tuberculosis as much as to the isolation and demoralisation that faced all revolutionary socialists in the im-mediate post-war period. But it permeates and finally vitiates an otherwise remarkable work. In some cases Orwell makes alterations which are quite easy to locate. The public execution is, for example, based on the famous case in December 1943 in Kharkov when three German members of the Gestapo and their Russian chauffeur were found guilty of operating mobile gas chambers. But there was in reality no blood lust. The (hopefully unadulterated) *Times* report noted that 'the crowd were not in lynching mood, for the majesty of the law deeply impressed them; for the second time in two years, there was joy in Kharkov'. Orwell once noted disparagingly of Jack London that one of his greatest literary skills was the portrayal of cruelty, an allegation of which he must himself surely stand indicted in *Nineteen Eighty-Four* .

The status of the 'book-within-the-book' is crucial in demon-strating the degree to which Orwell did the dirty on his own ideas. If the allusion here is to Trotsky's *Revolution Betrayed*, what Orwell must be saying (since the samizdat turns out to be O'Brien's fabrication) is that the only apparently truthful attempt at an account of the Soviet regime is just another pack of lies. This would accord with Orwell's stupid canard that 'Trotsky is as much responsible for the Russian dictatorship as any man now living'. So one of the most searching, consistent and personally courageous critics of Stalinism and Fascism becomes just another sell-out.

And the popular culture of 1984 is viewed as cynically as the political tracts, simply self-consoling worthless songs, machine written pulp fiction and tyrannical TV. For all his interest in mass culture, Orwell here inadvertently reveals the immense snobbery of the literary intellectual who automatically assumes that the post-war development of radio, television and pop music would be a debasing and pacifying influence. In fact these are forms within which quite sharp struggles are fought over meaning, and where visual and acoustic literacy has grown rather than been abolished – becoming focuses for resistance rather than agents of oppression. Here Orwell as the defender of the English language, scourge of abbreviation and partisan of sound spelling, was quite wrong. Rather than being a debased and restricted code, the modern English language, especially in its spoken and sung forms, has been immensely refreshed and expanded so that it is now more expressive and evocative than the strange argot in which so many 'lit. crits' conduct their affairs. It has after all been the reviled pop songs, such as *Anarchy in the UK*, *Ghost Town* and *Shipbuilding*, which have produced some of the finest and fiercest cries of defiance against the state of 1984. And he need not have feared for the abolition of history. Its preservation and rediscovery has become a national obsession, especially on the Left, contributing to our amnesia about the present.

But the greatest betrayal is in the portrayal of the proles. It has often been noted about Orwell's earlier journalistic work that he seemed almost to select the least organised, least conscious member of the working class to describe, and whom he could confidently disdain. But the proles of 1984 are quite without hope, not least because they have no involvement in the process of production. Although Orwell occasionally attributes to them an improbable penchant for insurrection, they are in reality suffocating in the comfortable decay of their cabbage smelling front room (Orwell's general sniffyness seems to verge on olfactory hallucination in these passages). Having deprived them of intellect, organisation and ambition, the tribute Orwell pays to their essential humanity seems a rather macabre consolation prize. As Raymond Williams puts it: '(Orwell) sees them as a shouting, stupid crowd in the street; drinking and gambling; like the ant which sees small subjects but not large ones, people who have never learnt to think. It is the world of working people, before 1914, as seen by the prep school boy ... if the tyranny of 1984 ever finally comes, one of the major elements in the ideological preparation will have been this way of "seeing the masses" '.

For despite the equally aloof intellectuals whose pessimistic prognostications clutter the modern Left wing press, what is most obvious is the growth, in size, social power, political consciousness and combativity of the modern working class. And what is most striking about the effect of even this mighty current depression is that the 'proles' as Orwell calls them are still prepared to down tools to defend a fellow who has been sacked for damaging a .72p mirror bracket or strike for weeks to retain the time to wash their hands before clocking off. In this world the phrase 'Big Brother is watching you' is a motto of defiance rather than a statement of resignation. And we can mark this same class in Poland and in Central America, and the township shanties of South Africa standing up together against forces of incomparable technical resources.

This is not a working class much loved by folklorists like Pahl or Seabrook who seem deliberately to avoid members of the working class who are working. It is too often white and male to be of much interest to the moralists of the libertarian Left. Yet to attempt to organise that potential for effective rebellion, in Orwell's own words 'a power that will one day overturn the world', remains the only real guarantee against 1984.

One is finally obliged to return for inspiration to Zamyatin's *We* – a greater novel in all respects – where the revolutionaries have organised a powerful party – the Mephi, almost space age Bolsheviks – rather than Orwell's defeated and domesticated proles. Zamyatin, active in the 1971 revolution, exiled by Stalin and a victim of censorship far more severe than Orwell ever experienced, pits the Mephi against the highly appropriate symbol of the State Rocket. There is a crucial exchange between a Mephi and a state mathematician, full of coded meaning for Russia in the 1920s. The mathematician argues that revolution within the system is impossible because 'our Revolution was the last'. The mocking reply of Zamyatin and the Mephi is very straightforward and very true: 'There is no ultimate revolution – revolutions are infinite in number.' It is in banishing that perspective, one which he had seen first hand in Barcelona and which had 'made me a socialist for the first time', that Orwell failed his last novel and his best self.

Chapter 3

Jenny Taylor
Desire is Thoughtcrime

In 1936, George Orwell concluded the first part of *The Road to Wigan Pier*, his documentary account of the condition of the northern working class, by evoking a 'memory of working class interiors – especially as I sometimes saw them in my childhood before the war, when England was still prosperous'. It was this picture, he stressed, '*not* the triumphs of modern engineering, nor the radio, nor the cinematograph ... that reminds me that our age has not altogether been a bad one to live in'. The image has become fixed in many more memories than Orwell's – steeped in nostalgia like a sepia photograph:

'Especially on winter evenings after tea, when the fire glows in the open range and dances mirrored in the steel fender, when Father, in shirt sleeves, sits in the rocking chair at one side of the fire reading the racing finals, and Mother sits on the other side with her sewing, and the children are happy with a penn'orth of humbugs and the dog lolls roasting himself on the rag mat – it is a good place to be in, provided that you can be not only in it but sufficiently *of* it to be taken for granted'.[1]

Privacy, cosiness, homeliness, a sense of belonging, of father, mother and children filling allotted positions; it is the diametrical opposite of the image of the future projected 12 years later in *Nineteen Eighty-Four*. Here, bleakness, coldness, combined dirt and sterility, the abolition of private spaces, are suggested by Winston Smith's dwelling, Victory Mansions, whose 'hallway smelt of boiled cabbage and old rag mats'. And it is confirmed by the dirt and disorder, both physical and social – children turning against parents, condoned by the state – of his neighbours, the Parsons' flat:

'Everything had a battered, trampled-on look, as though the place had just been visited by some large, violent animal. Games impedimentia – hockey sticks, boxing gloves, a burst football, a pair of sweaty shorts turned inside out – lay all over the floor, and on the table there was a litter of dirty dishes and dog-eared exercise books. On the wall were scarlet banners of the Youth League and the Spies and a full-sized poster of Big Brother. There was the usual boiled-cabbage smell, common to the whole building, but it was shot through with a sharper smell of sweat, which – one knew this at the first sniff, though it was hard to say how – was the sweat of some person not present at the moment. In another room some person with a comb and a piece of toilet paper was trying to keep tune with the military music which was still issuing from the telescreen.

"It's the children," said Mrs. Parsons, casting a half apprehensive glance at the door. "They haven't been out today ..." '[2]

The resonance of each of these pictures depends on the bringing together of a set of contrasts – of distance and desire, attraction and repulsion. In *The Road to Wigan Pier*, the cosy home of the Edwardian working class family operates primarily as a myth, curiously detached from the detailed accounts in the book of contemporary working class poverty. It is contrasted not so much with the strong – perhaps even romanticised – culture of the mining villages themselves, as with the dowdy, dirty, *out of placeness* of the gruesome Brookers' lodging house. Here the squalor of the surroundings – the dirty thumb print on the white bread, the full chamber pot under the dining room table – transgresses Orwell's boundaries of decency and thus both humanity and meaningful, historical, existence; it is 'some subterranean place where people go creeping round and round, just like blackbeetles, in an endless muddle of slovened jobs and mean grievances',[3] the same mean-ingless, brutalised squalor of the Parsons' flat. The different scenes are evoked and contrasted precisely because the narrative voice, the perceiving vision, is *in* it but not sufficiently *of* it to take it for granted. *In Nineteen Eighty-Four*, too, the political analysis works through setting up contrasts, and the narrative perspective is in but not sufficiently *of* the nightmare world that is being portrayed. But here a complex satirical process is in action.

This process works in three interconnected ways. Most clear is the development of Winston Smith, who is the 'Everyman' centre of consciousness in the novel, though not the narrator. Winston knows the horror of the situation both through immediate physical repulsion and by contrast with a range of mythic and individual memories and desires which serve both to make the present even more strange and horrible and to subvert it – though this is ultimately seen to be futile. Here the mythic past acts as Utopia – an 'ancestral memory that things had once been different.'[4] Secondly there is the process through which the power of the State – or simply of Power itself – is gradually realised, and which can ultimately only be made known to the reader through Winston's realisation of its ubiquitous force. The Party maxim which Winston contemplates fairly early in the book – 'Who controls the past controls the present; who controls the present controls the past' – is finally acted out on his own identity. Lastly there is the voice of the narrator, who simultaneously identifies with Winston and stands on one side and makes general comments, and who fills in deep background about the society to the reader. This voice provides a framework of decency and common sense within whose terms we read the novel. So the world of *Nineteen Eighty-Four* is shown to be unambiguously oppressive and unpleasant through reference to an unspoken set of assumptions built into the narrative perspective from the very first word. And it operates most powerfully in the setting up of a nexus of associations that bind together family loyalty, sexual relationships and male physical desire.

Here I want to explore the various ways that Orwell relates individual identity, family affection and sexuality in *Nineteen Eighty-Four*, and consider some of their political implications. And in some ways it is the very centrality of the relationship betwen sexual and political repression in *Nineteen Eighty-Four* that makes the novel seem so recognisable today. In others, it is what turns the book into a curio. But ultimately, *Nineteen Eighty-Four* fails to confront the complexity of the relationship between desire and patriarchal authority, sex and power. Fails, ironically, because on the surface it seems to be doing just that.

Orwell's conception of sexuality and human nature in *Nineteen Eighty-Four* is ambiguous. At first glance the notion of sexual repression and the potentially subversive role of desire seems to spring out of the Romantic idea of sexuality as a life force that emerges in different forms in the work of Blake and Shelly, Lawrence and Reich. But the novel is as much a critique as an affirmation of this tradition. As many critics have pointed out, its plot is almost identical to the Soviet novelist Zamyatin's *We*, written in 1923, a futuristic dystopia in which the hero D303 is moved by desire to political rebellion by the Other – E330 – though he finally betrays her. *Nineteen Eighty-Four* therefore needs to be read as a critical rewriting of Zamyatin's earlier book; as an extrapolation into Orwell's immediate future, our present, written in the context of the ideological assumptions surrounding sexuality and the family of Britain in the late 1940s[5]. Compared with *We*, however, and for all the talk of the importance of sex, *Nineteen Eighty-Four* is an almost completely unerotic novel, representing a curious mixture of rebellion and conservatism, prurience and prudishness.

England in Orwell's 1984 is a place of unrelieved sexual repression. This is not simply a by-product of the totalitarian regime but a precondition of its existence. In the upper world of Party functionaries sexual pleasure has been abolished, sex subordinated to reproduction, and in its place libidinal energy is channelled into physical sport – a sort of twentieth century totalitarian version of muscular Christianity – or (as in Reich's *The Mass Psychology of Fascism*) sublimated into love of Big Brother and hatred of Goldstein. This is made quite obvious, firstly by the narrator:

'The aim of the Party was not merely to prevent men and women forming loyalties which it might not be able to control. Its real, undeclared purpose was to remove all pleasure from the sexual act. Not love so much as eroticism was the enemy, inside marriage as well as outside it ... The only recognised purpose of marriage was to beget children for the service of the Party. Sexual intercourse was to be looked on as a slightly disgusting minor operation, like having an enema ... The sexual act, successfully performed, was rebellion. Desire was thought-crime.'[6]

And later this is developed by Julia: 'They want you to be bursting with energy all the time. All this marching up and down and cheering and waving flags is simply sex gone sour.'[7] Conversely, the nether world of the proles, glimpsed out of a corner of the eye, consists of a meaningless cycle of birth, copulation and death; a corrupted sexual hedonism is condoned, even encouraged, by the Party-controlled pornography industry.

Thus Winston's desire, and his doomed love affair with Julia, is neither free nor subversive but is always conditioned and determined by power. Yet the patterns of identification which are set up as you read the novel (at least for the first time) suggest something different. The narrative voice assumes empathy and complicity with Winston's adolescent schoolboy lust and confirms his projections of Julia, who thus functions both as an erotic fantasy and as a 'real' person. This emerges most forcefully in the yoking of violence and sexuality that characterises Winston's various fantasies and their subsequent enactment. At the beginning sexuality is totally pathologised. Winston uses his diary as a confessional, an attempt to speak about his pornographic encounter with the prole prostitute and thus to exorcise it: 'He had written it down at last, but it made no difference. The therapy had not worked. The urge to shout filthy words at the top of his voice was as strong as ever.'[8] On his first encounter with Julia, lust merges with hatred, desire is inseparable from violence; the libidinal energy that has been sublimated into hatred of Goldstein has been translated back into rape:

'Winston succeeded in transferring his hatred from the face on the screen to the dark-haired girl behind him. Vivid, beautiful hallucinations flashed through his mind. He would flog her to death with a rubber truncheon. He would tie her to a stake and shoot her full of arrows like Saint Sebastion. He would ravish her and cut her throat at the moment of climax. Better than before, moreover, he realised *why* it was that he hated her. He hated her because she was young and pretty and sexless, because he wanted to go to bed with her and would never do so, because round her sweet supple waist which seemed to ask you to encircle it with your arm, there was only the odious scarlet sash – aggressive symbol of chastity.'[9]

Conversely, the image of Julia also forms part of the pastoral myth of the 'ancient time', 'a time when there was privacy, love and friendship, and when members of a family stood by one another without needing to know the reason.' Here she is desexualised, linked with memories of his mother, the good breast, part of an Arcadian Golden age of plenitude:

'The girl with dark hair was coming towards them across the field. With what seemed a single movement she tore off her clothes and flung them disdainfully aside. Her body was white and smooth but it aroused no desire in him, indeed he barely looked at it. What overwhelmed him in that instant was admiration for the grace with which she had thrown her clothes aside. With its grace and carelessness it seemed to annihilate a whole culture, a whole system of thought, as though Big Brother and the Party and the Thought Police could all be swept into nothingness by a single splendid movement of the arm. That too was a gesture belonging to the ancient time. Winston woke up with the word 'Shakespeare' on his lips.'[10]

This dichotomy between lust and utopian desire, between woman as madonna and whore, is paradoxically both broken down and reinforced in Winston's love affair with the 'real' Julia. But both separately and together they act as escapist fantasies – as vacations rather than emancipations. In his first secret encounter with Julia in the hideout in the 'Golden Country' outside the city, Winston's desire is still negatively conditioned by the Party's puritanism, Julia's whorishness is simply the underside of repression; corruption is pleasurable only because it is corrupt: 'Not merely the love of one person, but the animal instinct, the simple undifferentiated desire – that was the force that would tear the Party to pieces.'[11] Later, undifferentiated sexuality is tempered by domesticity, the bug-infested room above the junk shop 'almost a home'. Julia remains a projection, but one who combines the characteristics of wife and whore, and in the process neither questions nor transgresses either category.

What are we to make of all this in the real 1984? Does the novel have anything useful to say about the links between sexual and political repression; the way that the relationship between sexuality, identity and power works today? In 1971, Raymond Williams considered the novel's treatment of sexuality to be the weakest aspect of *Nineteen Eighty-Four*. He wrote:

'Of the many failures of *Nineteen Eighty-Four* this is perhaps the deepest. All the ordinary resources of personal life are written off as summarily as the proles. The lonely fantasy of 'mighty loins' of the future is joined by the lonely confusion of the adolescent – so guilty about love – making that corruption of the object is a necessary element of its pleasure. Winston Smith is not like a man at all – in consciousness, in relationships, in the capacity for love and protection and endurance and loyalty. He is the last of the cut-down figures – less experienced, less intelligent, less loyal, less courageous than his creator – through whom rejection and defeat can be mediated.'[12]

But I would question whether the main failure of the novel really lies in not making Winston more of a 'real man' – a homely hero who could confidently transcend the tyranny within which he is caught. If for a moment you suspend disbelief and read the novel as I think Orwell intended – not as a literal or realistic prophesy, but as a speculative fiction concerning a society where coercive power is pushed to its absolute and logical conclusion, then it works, up to a point.

Within its own terms *Nineteen Eighty-Four is* convincing, not only as a fantasy of the ultimate form of totalitarianism, but of the ultimate form of patriarchy. By 'patriarchy' here I mean an essentially abstracted notion of male power as a force which pervades every aspect of the social structure, but which is always at some level reducible to violence. Within such a society it is imaginable that sexuality would be coded entirely through violence, that women would manifest themselves as either terrified downtrodden drudges like Mrs Parsons or as fetishised projections of male sexual obsessions and fears – Kathleen, Winston's frigid first wife on the one hand; Julia, 'intuitive' sexuality, whom Winston calls 'a revolutionary from the waist down', on the other. It is conceivable that Winston should experience his mother only as a sentimentalised absence, that he should feel an Oedipal ambivalence to the patriarchal authority manifested in the father figure O'Brien as well as hatred then love towards Big Brother, the more powerful sibling. But ironically the novel only works like this if it can do to the reader what the Party finally does to Winston Smith – draw one into its own self-referential world.

The world Orwell portrays is unconvincing as an imaginable society because there is no sort of dialectical process at work – it is outside history. The 'good life' with which the nasty present is compared is not only a nostalgic myth for Winston Smith – it has the same sort of fixed timelessness as the dominant regime. The power of the dominant order doesn't only control and thus brutalise the desire that attempts to subvert it. It fixes the real human capacities – love, solidarity, mutual aid, the possibility of critical, independent thought – back into a memory – into the picture of the enclosed Edwardian family of *The Road to Wigan Pier*; the image that somehow lies underneath Winston's lust (married love is as dangerous to the Party as casual sex). It locks these meanings and identifications into the privatised space of the nuclear couple, the closed room.

That is why *Nineteen Eighty-Four* remains such a powerful weapon for the Right in 1984. If you read it as a literal prediction of the structures of everyday life, then clearly Orwell got it wrong. For all the talk of 'Victorian Values' and the emphasis on the family under Thatcher, we are not heading for an age of sexual repression of the sort that Orwell describes. Furthermore, the model of sexual repression that he employs is unsatisfactory, with its conception of sexuality as an 'essential force' to be kept down. Oddly enough there is a sense in which sexuality in *Nineteen Eighty-Four* and what Orwell elsewhere calls the 'dirty handkerchief side of life',[13] is outside power as well as being determined by it. Just as Orwell could not see the potential of capitalism to develop a highly sophisticated consumer economy while maintaining an escalating arms production; so he could not anticipate how sexuality would become the apotheosis of commodity fetishism. Sexuality always tends to be bound up with power relations within the social structure (and this is not confined to capitalism, either contemporarily or historically), with patterns of domination and subordination. But does this process work simply through repression, which implies that there is something already there to be repressed? I would argue that it operates more profoundly in structuring the forms of desire itself – in what we want and how we want it. Paradoxically, the periods we think of as times of great sexual repression, such as the nineteenth century, are moments when there is a far greater degree of consciousness about sexuality than before, and when sexuality itself comes to be emphasised as the 'truth' of the individual.[14]

The novel is thus not so much an anticipation of future trends as an expression of the half shameful, half salacious sense of the sexual in 1948. This also means that its author couldn't have conceived of sexual politics as it has been posed by the Women's Movement. Although sex is seen as an act of rebellion in the novel, at the same time it is depoliticised. I am sure that if Orwell had lived to see contemporary feminism he would have loathed it – at least his remarks about alternative cultural forms: like the 'middle class socialists, feminists, cranks and vegetarians' in *The Road to Wigan Pier*, suggest as much. Yet there is a great deal of common ground between aspects of Orwell and the aspirations of socialist feminism. Each shares a suspicion of centralised forms of political organisation, a dislike for overblown political jargon; they both emphasise that to be successful socialism must connect with people's everday experience and at the same time construct a new common sense through which that experience can be understood.

As I write this, in the summer of 1983, in anticipation of 1984, this morning's papers bring news of the government's decision to cut £1 billion from State spending, and to send troops to 'protect' the cruise missile base from the women protesters of Greenham Common. Both are being done, through a perverse and twisted logic, in the name of 'freedom'. That concept of freedom has been able to sustain a measure of popular support in this country by binding together a collection of associations – patriotism, family loyalty, responsibility – and make them seem aspects of a meaningful whole. Thatcherism has taken the positive emotions of love of place, resolution in the face of adversity, desire for independence, self respect, and linked them to destructive aggression, nationalism, to a Darwinian 'survival of the fittest' idea of social organisation; and above all, to ideological hostility to all forms of state intervention, combined with increasing actual state surveillance and control. In the political climate leading up to and in 1984, words are not being abolished as in Newspeak, but their meanings are subtly shifting. This is happening most sharply in the implications of the ways that the ambiguous concepts of 'public' and 'private' are set up in opposition to each other. 'Private' derives one set of meanings from being one side of dichotomy that was consolidated during the first half of the nineteenth century. Within this framework it connotes homeliness, mutual aid, warmth, security against the harsh, competitive and impersonal world of work. This dichotomy tends to drain positive meaning from 'public', which comes to connote bareness and bleakness – the stripping away of close, personal association. Yet there are other, older, meanings of 'public'. There is the fundamental sense of 'public' as 'of or pertaining to the people as a whole, that belongs to, or affects or concerns the community or nation; common, national, popular'.[15] Here the meaning of public is bound up with collective identity, community, citizenship, the general will and common well being, as well as with the symbolic formation of the nation. This moves into the sense of public as meaning 'Done or made by or on behalf of the community as a whole; authorised by, acting for or representing the community'. This liberal, democratic sense of public as expressing or representing the will of the people transfers more negative meaning to 'private', binding it up with concepts of exclusivity, lack of accountability, self-seeking profiteering. One of the ways that Thatcherism works is to invest the 'private' of private enterprise with all the connotations of close personal ties, and stripping 'public' of all suggestion of the general will and turning it, negatively, into impersonal bureaucracy, positively, linking it with a constructed tradition of patriotic ceremonial.

Of course it is not that simple. The public sphere has not become a negative space purely through some plot of Thatcher's or the power of language alone, and to suggest as much would be artificially to amplify Thatcherism's ideological influence. It stems in part from the real failures in public policy and state controlled welfare which has characterised successive Labour and Conservative governments in the post-war period; and it affects people's real experience of those state institutions. Orwell's *Nineteen Eighty-Four is* at some level an extrapolation of some of our worst fears of the way that state controlled institutions might invade and control personal life. Yet at the same time it is no accident that during the 1979 Election campaign one of the Tory posters read: 'Where will you be after five years of Labour Government? In 1984'. I am sure that if Orwell was still alive today he would be playing a vital role in building a socialist alternative to Thatcherism. He would have been even more horrified at the uses that *Nineteen Eighty-Four* has been put to than he was before he died in 1950. Nevertheless, and irrespective of Orwell's intention, the novel is more likely to be effective in contributing to the attack on the public sphere than in increasing the resistance to the trend towards authoritarianism in contemporary British society. 'Who controls the past controls the future; who controls the present controls the past.' There will be a large print run of *Nineteen Eighty-Four* in 1984. Let us hope that three years hence, on the fiftieth anniversary of the Spanish Civil War, there will be a demand for an even larger print run of *Homage to Catalonia.*

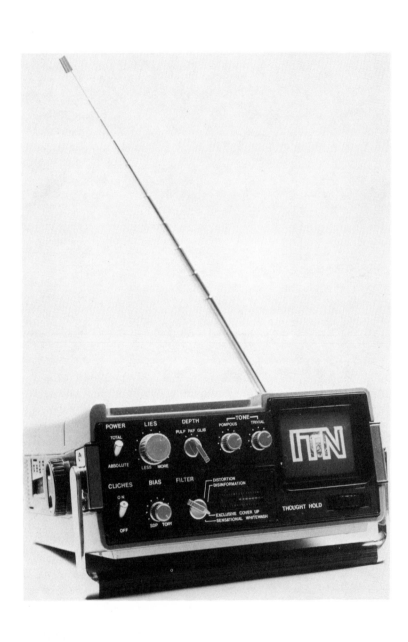

Chapter 4

Paul Chilton
Newspeak: It's The Real Thing

1. A Fragment

There was nothing official about newspeak in 1984; nor was there anything particularly new about it. There was nothing official, that is, in the sense of public functionaries devising new grammatical forms, coining new words and defining new meanings. It was, however, the case that the manner of speaking and writing practised by state agencies, such as the Departments of Employment, Health, Social Security and Defence – whose real business had more to do with unemployment, illness, insecurity and war – was domineering, deceptive, and sometimes difficult to understand.

It was also the case that the ruling section of the population was able to hire the services of professional 'language manipulators' to supplement its own linguistic domination, and that the newer techniques of electronic communication provided the means of propagating such carefully packaged messages. The tacit aim of those in power was to gain popular support by circulating, through the medium of the radio, the television and the newspaper, a restricted set of thoughts and mental attitudes consistent with their own way of seeing the world. Since speech was the key to this end, the intention was to make speech, and especially speech on any subject not ideologically neutral, as nearly as possible independent of critical consciousness. This ensured that the desired feelings and ideas would be received and passed around. The practice has been called 'duckspeak' by the writer George Orwell.

It was always possible to turn off the radio set and the television screen, but it was normal for many people to keep one or the other switched on during the day and evening. In many workplaces, even in those where the noise from machinery was considerable, but especially in the quieter domestic workplace (where most women worked), the radio would throughout the day be broadcasting a continuous flow of 'newsitems', advertisements and other entertainments, the categories sometimes merging into one another. If you had a radio or 'telly', you were defined as a 'listener' or 'viewer', or both, and listen and view was what you felt you should do. They were, apart from the newspapers, which took up a lot of time and space, the only way of hearing about the outside world and about the decisions made by people in remote places concerning your life and livelihood.

The people who made the decisions were not themselves 'viewed' directly, but 'inter-viewed', and even on those programmes where people 'appeared' to put questions to politicians, controls could be exercised by the 'chair person' (a popular euphemism for chairman), who might wish to maintain a 'balanced view' (that is an uncritical view), or might wish to create dramatic effect, or what was professionally called 'good television'. The television was nevertheless regarded with almost superstitious respect: to have 'seen it on the telly' was considered by many people to be a guarantee of factual truth. A 'telly' was a machine which told you things, like an oracle; one special service of newsitems and other information was even called by that ancient Greek name. And whatever other potential distractions existed, the common feeling was, you might as well watch it, you might as well get your money's worth.

It was a bright warm day in June, and the digital clock on the kitchen wall discreetly clicked 1325. Smythe jerked his way through the glass door of his living room. A face on the large flat televisionscreen, which he had recently been persuaded to have hung comfortably near his heating bars, glanced at him with direct eyes against a background of dark blue drapes. A young woman, who was presumably his wife, was sitting with her back to him and seemed to be agreeing with everything that the face was saying. 'I think you are *so* right, I do *so* agree with you,' he heard her say in a rather silly feminine voice. The other voice never stopped. It was low in pitch, reassuring, yet sporadically urgent, as if to alert anyone listening to a danger they had failed to notice. It was difficult to pick out from the stream of speech any clear argument or facts, but the smooth contours of the unbroken sentences threw certain phrases into relief.

Strong in belief ... resolute in our action ... hold firmly together ... freedom and justice ... sacred flame of liberty ... future belongs to free democracies ... new birth of freedom ... preserve our civilisation ...

What was so soothing to Smythe was the euphony of the speech, which seemed to outweigh all other considerations. The sentences were intoned without a hesitation or a falter in a solid string of verbal chunks. The regularity of grammar was of no consequence, and the usual means of expressing and assessing truth – likelihood, cause, the time of an event, these seemed to be unimportant and were submerged beneath the fluent rhythm. The stuff that was coming out of the mouth of the face on the televisionscreen consisted of words, but it was not speech in the true sense: it was a noise uttered without active thought, like the quacking of a duck. It was not the brain that was speaking, it was the larynx.

And the larynx spoke to the gut, provoking the secretion of those *hormones associated with courage, fear, pride and resolve. It was all done by repetition – not merely of the same words, but by the repetition of bits of meaning implied by words which were physically different:* **strong, firm, hold.** *Simultaneously, the emotions of vague collective security were stimulated:* **our, together;** *and in case all this evoked too static or complacent a mood, the promise of purpose and prospect was excited by bits of meaning spinning away from* **action, future, new birth.** *But such emotions could only make sense to Smythe if they were set against still stronger ones: the fear of alien forces, and the will to defend one's homeland. To speak of* **preserving our civilisation** *made sense only if there was some threat to preserve it against, a threat from some alien power which was the very antithesis of civilisation. The threat was most effectively invoked when it was left generalised, and Smythe experienced a vague spasm of hate connected with subversives, extremists, marxists, militants and pacifists, none of whom could be thought of as part of the majority of decent, moderate, realistic and law-abiding people in this country. The word* **civilisation,** *on the other hand, was joined to other verbal lumps made up of nouns cemented by sound:* **Freedom-n-justice, freedomocracies.** *They poured forth, like a line of type cast solid; and it was widely accepted that these were* **good** *things, approved of by all right-thinking people, and that for the moment it was the Conservative Party that possessed them. It was also generally expected that everyone would cheer, at least inwardly, whenever they heard these words, although 'cheer' is perhaps too profane a term, since the emotion they were capable of arousing was almost religious. It was* **belief** *that was supposed to make you strong, and* **a new birth** *of a* **sacred flame** *that was meant to inspire you in a prophetic vision of the* **future.**

Such curiously impressive performances, in which sight and sound could conspire to obscure logical meaning, were not uncommon on the televisionscreen. The odd thing was, Smythe thought, the way those eyes looked constantly round the audience, while the voice never stopped to correct itself, or to allow its brain time to plan the next sentence. It could not have been reading from a script, because the eyes never looked down. For a moment Smythe wondered whether **his** *brain had been mistaken, perhaps through fatigue, in not classifying this as drama-documentary (sometimes known as 'faction') with an actor memorising a script, or perhaps as a 'commercial'. But it did not seem likely, and the only explanation was that the performer's brain was, in some sense, not at the time fully in control of what it was saying. You had the feeling that this was not a real human being, but some kind of dummy.*

The true explanation, unknown at that time to Smythe, lay in an ingenious piece of electronic technology. It was called the 'Sincerity Machine', and had been pioneered, as he himself would no doubt have put it, by the ageing president of Oceania, a former actor in popular films about cowboys. The thing had been admiringly adopted by the Conservative Leader of Airstrip One. It consisted of a transparent plastic lectern onto which a hidden projector cast the text of a speech. Because of the angle of the lectern the text remained invisible to everyone except the speaker, and the PR (Public Relations) experts, who controlled the device on back-stage television monitors. The speaker could read the words without looking down or hesitating – actions which were associated with weakness, uncertainty and evasiveness – while appearing to be speaking with spontaneous honesty and conviction.

To the viewer, Smythe, these seemingly minor changes in the complex of subtle signals that make up the act of communication were capable of changing the nature of political 'dialogue'. The new smoothly produced performance conferred a distinct dramatic quality: the speaker could now appear as a protagonist in a heroic piece of theatre on the world stage. Disbelief could be suspended. The only difference was that this was real life.

2. Control

The rhetorical techniques for influencing and controlling others through language were probably widely developed in Europe in the Greek democracies. The subsequent invention of print then made it that much easier to manipulate public opinion, and the film and radio carried the process further. By the dawn of 1984 the development of television, and other forms of electronic media, means that mass communication, both verbal and visual, is more pervasive and persuasive than ever before.

This technical potential for control must be set against ideas of how language work, notably those whose theories of the differences in linguistic practice between working class and middle class speakers of English have emphasised how language can define and reinforce the social hierarchy. Bernstein is often interpreted to be talking about accent, especially the accent of the economically dominant South East, which is the accent spoken by those who attended certain educational institutions, and therefore the accent of national power, prestige and authority. This has also become the accent of broadcasting. In fact, the core of Bernstein's theory[1] is his distinction between a 'restricted code' spoken by some people and an 'elaborated code' spoken by others. 'Restricted code' was supposed to be the use of simple sentences, limited and inexplicit means of referring to things, lack of abstractions and lack of self-reference. Bernstein thought that working class children used this in schools, where 'elaborated code' was expected, and thus did poorly; he also concluded that 'restricted code' led to restricted ability to form concepts.

Orwell's Newspeak as Fowler and Hodge[2] point out, looks very like Bernstein's 'restricted code'. It has reduced complexity, few abstractions, and no self-reference creating the conditions for self-criticism. But it is also a restricted code peculiar to the ruling class; the proles do not speak it. Its purpose is to provide a medium of expression for the world view and ideology of the ruling elite, and also to make all other modes of thought impossible. And if it has an equivalent in the real 1984, it is to be found in the rhetoric of party politics, the bureaucratic prose of the agents of the state, and the arcane incantations of those who are cast in the role of 'experts'. No one can force you to speak or write this language, but its ubiquitous broadcast creates a pressure to employ it simply in order to communicate economically.

The political scientist Murray Edelman has explained this potential political role for the Bernstein dichotomy.[3] Bernstein is wrong, he argues, to correlate an 'elaborated' language with class level,[4] and sees the cruder formulations of this view as a classification scheme with two political functions: to reinforce the consignment of people to different levels of merit; and to justify controls over them. The Edelman dichotomy is between a formal, elaborated language capable of calling attention to factual allegations and logical relationships, and of expressing alternative views of reality, and a public language which 'validates established beliefs and strengthens the authority structure of the policy or the organisation in which it is used.'[5] This latter tends to be a 'tough' language, discouraging the verbalisation of tender (or 'wet') feelings. It takes many forms, of which the appeal to patriotism and support for the leader and her or his regime are but the most obvious.

The basic tendency of 'restricted public language' in Edelman's sense is to close off discourse, allowing only certain topics to be discussed, to obscure references to causation or responsibility, and to disallow criticism. These ends are achieved by linguistic means. It may seem strange that anyone should get away with such things. The fact is, however, that the political culture of 1984, underpinned by the press and the electronic media, privileges a certain 'voice'.

The nature of this Institutional Voice (IV) has been analysed by Claire Lindegren Lerman, who has given the term 'topic trans-formation' to its techniques of reality control.[6] The IV does not speak in its own personal capacity, but equates itself with its office or role, rather like the royal 'we'. It identifies its policies with 'the good of all', 'national security', 'public interest', 'our way of life' and so forth. It alone has the right to speak for the nation or institution; it is the repository of power and tradition; and it makes a unique claim to virtue. It thus has the ability to define events and people, and to assign a moral value to them. The IV accomplishes this by transforming the topics of discourse, by modifying or suppressing irksome political topics like unemployment, the nuclear arms race, the motives of the Falklands war. Its most powerful linguistic tools are much like those of Edelman's public language, but can now be spelled out in more detail: 1. the choice of grammatical constructions that avoid explicit reference to causes, agent, time and place; 2. the preference for and production of particular words, plus the preference for and production of particular metaphors, hiding some aspects of a reality and heightening others; 3. the invitation to draw inferences as a consequence of 1 and 2, evoking wider patterns of unspoken belief. All three of these linguistic practices are exemplified in what follows.

It's a beautiful thing, the destruction of words. So said Syme in *Nineteen Eighty-Four*, busily working on the crude dictionary of Newspeak. In 1984, topic control is subtler, but the aim is the same: 'Don't you see that the whole aim of Newspeak is to narrow the range of thought?'[7] The campaign against CND in 1983, for example, involved a systematic attempt to replace the term 'unilateral' in public debate with the term 'one-sided', thus implying intellectual and moral limitation. The ultimate achievement for the IV, however, would be to get its vocabulary imperceptibly incorporated into popular use. The word 'deterrent' is almost such a case. It has long been in public usage, and encapsulates a whole ideology based on the simultaneous evocation of threat and reassurance. Even the form of the word gives it a technical connotation, and therefore a kind of authority. But what is most important is that the term 'deterrent' carries unspoken implications: firstly it says, in military contexts, 'nuclear', without saying it outloud; secondly, it asserts, as if it were a fact, that A deters B; and thirdly, it says that B is aggressive and A is non-aggressive so the word asserts the presence of an alien threat while at the same time promising the ability to ward it off. It is thus a potent symbol for attracting political allegiance, and whose usefulness becomes clear in the course of public debate, where to say 'It is wrong to want to get rid of the deterrent' is almost self-evidently true.

Is it simply a coincidence that the other domain in which the word 'deterrent' is used is of that public order (the 'rope') and school discipline ('the cane')? 'The deterrent' and hanging are still synonymous – of course people still have to say 'I believe hanging to be a deterrent'. But the beliefs in the two deterrents, the rope and the bomb, are symmetrical and intimately related. The one wards off internal evil and the fear of disorder, the other external evil and the fear of invasion. And the link between these two can sometimes surface in curious ways.

An article with the telling title 'The Front Line against Youth Unemployment' (*Daily Telegraph*, 19 July, 1982) treats the problem of the jobless as an internal evil[8] to be 'combatted'. The 'front line' in question turns out to be a secondary modern school for girls in Chatham, and the ensuing discourse shows how linguistic cues can trigger off interconnected beliefs concerning the economy, defence and public order. ' "We are trying," declared the headmistress, a Mrs Dagger, "to turn out [the pupils = products on an assembly line] the sort of people who will exhibit [not really *have* of course] middle-class notions of what is acceptable [to whom?] and marketable." ' The author of the article also comments: 'It's the schools who are marketing a product'. Now the metaphor 'headmistress' is not applied to the Prime Minister in 1984 for nothing; nor are war, work and school, captains of companies, captains of industry and captains of schools verbally connected for nothing. For in the Chatham girls' school, marketing is a military operation and teaching is indoctrination. Economic war justifies draconian measures. 'Part of the process [the education of children = the processing of products] is simple, unrelenting [this word is second cousin to 'resolute'] *brainwashing* (my italics) ... ' The senior master, described by the article's author as 'the market economy made flesh', has more powerful 'weapons' at his disposal, however. There is an interesting progression from seeing education as an industrial process to seeing it as psychological warfare, and finally as physical warfare. The military-industrial-educational complex, in fact. 'The brainwashing,' we are told, 'is backed up by an old-fashioned system of discipline with a considerable range of minor punishments,' and Mr Market-economy-made-flesh, the senior master, is even quoted as adding ('with a grin') – 'up to nuclear weapons'.

Such things can be laughed off, and the article taken as satire. But suppose it is not. Vocabulary, metaphor and implications all work to organise a highly partial view of reality. The discourse is built round the threat or fear of unemployment; this is linked with the fear of youth and of domestic discourse; and this in turn with the fear of alien threat. The unifying, and wholly irrational, resolution to this cluster of phobias is the symbol of the 'deterrent' as safeguard and discipline. And although this is a media message, the speaker is none-the-less the Institutional Voice.

A more obvious operation of the IV can be seen in face-to-face utterances, like a radio interview (BBC Radio 4, 17 April, 1980) in which the Prime Minister demonstrated control of the topic of trade unions:

'I'm not afraid of the trade unions [breath] which carry out the True ideal of trade unions, which is to get to a Fair return for their members ... and to help to raise the prosperity of the country. Because the *fact is* that the only group of people in this country who are above the law in some respects *is* the trade unions.

... Indeed the majority of them [trade union members] don't like it. We want to reduce the power of *the militants* in the trade unions to use the unions to *their* advantage, and not to the advantage of the country.'[9]

The IV conventionally has the right to make such claims to the truth. Hence, 'the true ideal ... *is*', 'the only group ... *is*', 'indeed', and above all 'the fact *is*'. In fact, a frequent feature of this speaker's discourse is the expression 'you know', implying superior knowledge on her part. The IV defines threats to the national security. Hence, the unions are represented as something of which one might be afraid, though the IV reassuringly asserts its own fearlessness. It is implied that there exist false unions, distinct from the 'true' ones (in 1983 ministers also made claims about the '*true* peace movement'); and they are 'the militants', they have 'power' that they use 'not to the advantage of the country'. The IV claims virtue as well as the truth: it knows what is 'fair'. Typically it claims to know 'public opinion' and to be aligned with it: 'the majority of them'.

The IV's control of difficult topics by appeal to national security and patriotism was clearly seen when it was questioned on television during the 1983 election. The difficult topic was whether it had been necessary during the Falklands war of 1982 to torpedo an Argentinian cruiser called the Belgrano. Being dissatisfied with the Prime Minister's evasive answer, the questioning member of the electorate committed the unpardonable fault of challenging the IV's virtue and veracity by saying: 'That's not good enough, Mrs Thatcher'. To this the IV replied by suppressing the difficult topic and transforming it into an indirect assertion of the identity between the IV's actions and the national interest: ' ... only in England could anybody question the sinking of an *enemy* ship'. The factual details were replaced by the symbolic opposition of 'England' and the stressed 'enemy', the linguistic construction presenting the event as a timeless phenomenon beyond moral questioning.

The Falklands war was indeed a case where the IV, with the support of the media, effectively ruled criticism off-side, together with any link between that war and the economic and political situation at home. This is not to say that 'free speech' itself was suppressed, merely that dissent was drowned by the Institutional Voice. The war itself was not necessary: it was a symbol in political discourse. As Orwell's Goldstein wrote: 'The war, though it is unreal is not meaningless. It eats up the surplus of consumable goods, and it helps to preserve the typical mental atmosphere that a hierarchical society needs ... the object of war is not to make or prevent conquests of territory, but to keep the structure of society intact.'[10] Preventing conquest of territory was precisely the ostensible reason for the Falklands war. But its real function was to enable the IV to assert its own rightness by invoking an alien threat, by branding as 'traitors' people who voiced objections, and by perversely defining warfare as 'work' – 'just doing one's job'. Government and media rhetoric at the time of the railwaymen's strike, which occurred shortly after the war, was a mirror image of the Falklands reaction.[11]

What the above examples show is not the power of a neo-Newspeak to control thought. They show rather that in political discourse language is used to define and redefine reality for the advantage of a dominant ideology. It may be that many people are induced to accept some or all of the messages conveyed, but that is not a necessary consequence. Thought and language are not necessarily identical. What is more, language has the peculiar property of being able to refer to itself, so that any linguistically realised version of reality is capable of turning on itself.

3.   Ubo: Another fragment

*'This business of petty inconvenience and indignity, of being kept waiting about, of having to do everything at other people's convenience, is inherent in working-class life. A thousand influences constantly press a working man down into a **passive** role.'*[12] *Or rather an unworking man, thought Smythe, as he stood in the queue, reading Leaflet NI-12. From this he discovered that there were a limited number of people involved in the situation in which he found himself: 'me', 'them', 'the wife', 'the dependants', and perhaps an 'employer'; a limited number of things: 'money', 'work', 'tax'; in a limited number of places: 'the Jobcentre'; and limited (or was it to be unlimited?) periods of time: 'days', 'weeks', 'months', 'years'. But there was more than that to the leaflet. There was another, disembodied anonymous voice addressing you, pigeon-holing you, expecting you to do things, and giving orders.*
   [YOU WILL BE ASKED.]

It was impossible and meaningless to query 'by whom'? How else could it be said? It was in the nature of the relationship between the authorities and Smythe in his present position that the process should be grammatically passive. This feeling of being the powerless subject of actions performed by anonymous agents grew as Smythe read on. He did not act, he was acted upon. He felt himself the slave of mysterious authority; he felt that 'they' would never allow him to do this, that and the other.

[*YOU ARE REQUIRED, YOU ARE NOT REQUIRED, YOU ARE UNEMPLOYED, YOU WILL BE GIVEN, YOU CAN BE SENT, YOU ARE EXPECTED* ...] In spite of the repeated 'you', he began to feel that he did not know who he, that is 'you' was, any more than he knew the identity of 'them'. There was no doubt that he was the 'you' intended in the phrase 'you lose your job', but was he a 'you' who could enrol in the awesome PER? It was all very well to know what this stood for, but acronyms had a habit of taking on a life of their own. And the next sentence required a different kind of mental effort:

'... you will not be required to register for work unless you are under 18 years old, but you can still make use of your local Jobcentre ...

This was not perhaps as difficult to decipher as the sentence 'It is not the case that negative sentences are not harder to understand than affirmatives', but it did take more time to make sense of than saying 'If you are under 18, you will be required ...'

The well-dressed woman in front of Smythe was sweating slightly. Was she a 'you', he asked himself. It occurred to him that 'you' was in itself normally genderless, but could turn masculine or feminine depending on surrounding words. 'Neighbour', for example, became feminine when you said 'my neighbour is pregnant', and so it did, for slightly different reasons, if you said 'my neighbour is doing the washing'. He had a feeling that 'you' in the Ubo was always assumed to be masculine. 'If your wife stops working,' spoke the voice in the leaflet, and there was no way of knowing that this 'you' could be any different from the 'you' in the other sentences. If she stops working, what then? 'You ... claim extra benefit **for her**,' replied the voice. If both husband and wife were out of work, then the man claimed. But what if a woman was unemployed and unmarried? What, for that matter, if she was married? The voice did not, apparently, speak to such persons.

The queue was moving slowly, and Smythe preferred this game to chess problems. The first sentence now said, 'you (man) **lose your job**,' the later one 'your wife **stops working**'. Wives who stopped working were, it now seemed, part of some uncontrollable thing happening, referred to as 'your (men) circumstances chang[ing]'. Smythe's pulse quickened as he glimpsed still more possible messages; the train of his *thoughts was, he knew, unacceptable, unreasonable, but he did not stop short.*

'You lose your job ... your wife stops working'. Lose: did that mean lose like losing an arm, or lose like losing your hat, by being damn careless? At any rate, it implied you didn't intend to do it. It seemed that they expected 'you' (man) would become unemployed because something happened (even though you might be blamed for being lazy, stupid or imprudent), while wives 'stopped working' because ... well, because they intended to, wanted to. You men were expected to have a job; your wives could, it was implied, choose whether they had one or not. It also occurred to him, as he allowed his thoughts to drift, that if you did think of 'stop working' as something just happening, then you had to think of the wife as a kind of mechanical gadget that had ceased to function.

A shuffling in the queue brought him back to the question of his relationship to 'them'. The leaflet's Big Brotherly voice said, but somehow said it without saying it, that Smythe, the woman in front and every you in the Ubo, was to take on the role of receiving orders (as well as 'benefits'). The disembodied voice rapped out the commands: GO ... GIVE ... DO NOT DELAY ... FILL IT IN ... RETURN IT QUICKLY ... ASK ... READ IT ... MAKE SURE ... FOLLOW ... TELL THE BENEFIT OFFICE EVERYTHING YOU ARE REQUIRED TO ...]

*There was also a prediction of Smythe's future actions in the office, a prediction which he knew he must fulfill: 'Each time you claim benefit, you will sign that you have read and understood UBL 18. So read it ...'. Not only would he sign, he **would** read, and he **would** understand; if he was going to sign, he **must** be going to read, he **must** be going to understand. He longed for this understanding. The woman was already reading the inside of UBL 18, and on its front Smythe saw* **So you must tell us at once. You must tell us immediately.** *Imperatives, which are after all just verbs with 'you' suppressed, are full of power, mused Smythe, beginning to penetrate the labyrinthine language game.*

*What else could you, and they, do with verbs? If imperatives were anything to go by, you ought to be able to indicate whether an action was enforced or permitted, possible or impossible, real or unreal, likely or unlikely. Smythe had not thought of cans, mights, mays, woulds and shoulds in quite this light before, but those were clearly the words involved. Certainly the distinction between having the ability to do something and being allowed to do it was sometimes not very clear in this system. 'Payment **cannot** be backdated': it was just one of those petty inconveniences about payments. 'You **can** be sent to prison' meant of course that 'we (or they) can send you', but they wrote it so that it seemed to be just one of those inherent inconveniences about **you**. They had another way of implying what they thought about you, which made* *use of phrases beginning with 'if': 'if you tell a lie', for instance, seemed to suppose that you were likely to.*

*Almost all the verbs, Smythe noticed, had a can, may or might carefully connected to them, presumably to avoid definite commitment on the part of the authorities. This was scarcely reassuring, since any apparent offer of rights was instantly hedged. Even if it was 'very difficult' for you to 'attend' the Ubo ('attendance' was a duty normally expected of church-goers and schoolchildren), the most they offered was that 'you **may** be able to claim by post'. Could Smythe, who had cycled ten miles and left his small son with a neighbour, have stayed at home or not? 'If you don't claim', it was not clear what might happen: 'you **may** lose your money'. Only they could decide.*

*The obligations of the Ubo certainly weren't clear, but what, he wondered, were **his** obligations? Smythe read the front of UBL 18 with difficulty, as he and the woman moved toward the counter. **Responsibilities of Claimants**. 'This leaflet tells you', said the Institutional Voice. 'Read it ... If you break the rules [as you are likely to], you **may** be breaking the law ... These are the rules, but if you are not sure whether you should **tell** us about something, **tell** us anyway, just in case. You should read it and remember ... .'*

*He should have known, of course, that the general rules would be indicated, but not the law, for what counted was right thinking. One should not only have the right opinions, but the right instincts. Yes, he would tell Big Brother all, he would tell him that he had read and understood, and that he had also not understood; he would tell him that he filled his memory with dos, don'ts, coulds and shoulds, but that at the end of it all he knew only that he must TELL. But he had already gone too far. He was losing the faculty of stopping short at the threshold of dangerous thoughts, the power of **not** grasping analogies; he was forgetting how to **fail** to perceive logical errors, how to **misunderstand** the simplest arguments that were not moderate, he was forgetting how to be bored or repelled by trains of thought which were not sensible, reasonable and orthodox.*

Chapter 5

Florence Lewis & Peter Moss
The Tyranny of Language

– 1 –

George Orwell's *Nineteen Eighty-Four* has two large, encompassing thematic principles – the development and the imaginative uses of manipulation and suppression. Airstrip One and Oceania are not simply administered and controlled by the Inner Party; they and their inhabitants are *created* by the ruling group, which imposes private and public patterns of discrimination. These include the abolition and destruction of ancestral, historical and personal memories in favour of approved cultural and social doctrine; the destruction of natural language in favour of codified forms of communication; and the denial of spontaneous feelings and love in favour of orchestrated, official rituals. These are regular way-stations which the inhabitants of Oceania are required to visit [by the Party] en route to the ultimate destination of Thought-Control.

These imposed discriminations are not part of Western culture in the gross forms in which Orwell displays them, largely because democratic societies still have powerful constraints which inhibit such practices. However, manipulation and suppressions of a different but similar order *are* widespread in the democracies, as is the ease with which powerful minorities impose their ways of seeing, or not seeing, upon contemporary societies.

Mass media are the channels which carry information and fiction in both the real and imaginary 1984, and it's instructive to observe the resemblances in official material. In the novel, the major technological medium, the telescreen, delivers regular, if sometimes unexpected, catalogues of achievements: economic targets met; military victories won; presents ritualistic participatory dramas: the hate sessions directed at enemies of the State; and transmits interminable, banal songs. Our main technological medium, television, has more surface variety and presents evidence of tension and disagreement in social and cultural life rather than the grey sameness of Oceania. However, at a deeper level the medium's styles and codes, in both worlds, are similar; and both are powered by the conventions of theatre. Oceania's language styles are breathless, even febrile, and its themes located in the theatre of cruelty; our television codes are more subtle but the range is not much greater.

Consider these examples. News and current affairs programmes are predicated upon the dramatic requirement of climax and release; interview styles are generally confrontationist, seeking effect. Discussions on political and economic matters avoid clear presentation of issues or a probing for possible solutions, erecting instead edifices of conventional attitudes built upon an obscuring rhetoric. Even general, relaxing entertainment is constructed ideologically. Recall the sub-theme in *Edward VII* of the creation of Royalty as human, understandable and necessary. Or take *Yes Minister* with its facile comic dramatisation of the battle between Bureaucracy and Representative Democracy. In America we have the F. Lee Bailey show, wherein men and women accused of a crime can demonstrate their innocence by submitting to a lie detector test on national television. Thus, a matron who insists that the late Elvis Presley was the father of her 21-year-old son learns from her polygraph that he was not. And one of the Watergate burglars is cleared of the charge that he was part of a plot to assassinate John F. Kennedy. In which direction does sanity and responsibility lie when in less than two minutes on television a man [involved in illegal activity with the C.I.A.] establishes his essential credibility? Our television is nearer black comedy than the theatre of cruelty, but the central mind-deflecting mechanisms are the same as those on Orwell's telescreens.

Technically, also, this medium is used in similar ways in both 'worlds'. At the beginning of the novel, Orwell describes a hate session against the ubiquitous enemy, Goldstein. Parts of the telefilm are controlled by fast dissolves and double images in order to produce a variety of audience reactions. Camera angles and variable lighting are also widely used in contemporary studio formats to 'aid' interpretation. A recent study of the award-winning and widely popular major American CBS current affairs programme *Sixty Minutes* showed how judgements, made by the producers about the moral or ethical status of interviewers, are signalled by viewers by simple visual clues:

'A producer who has worked on *Sixty Minutes* says that on more than one occasion he watched Mike Wallace (a star reporter) record an interview during which Wallace smiled and encouraged the subject to continue talking, only to insert cutaways in which Wallace has a stern, doubting expression.'[2]

The programme uses production techniques which appear to heighten the ethos of the reporters while undermining that of the subjects. The reporters and the interviewers are therefore seen as strong, assertive, dominating and wholly credible. All of this achieves the strong suggestion of a trusted source of information. A benign but firm big brother.

If we use Orwell's 'Big Brother' as a symbol for pervasive knowledge, then the media in 1984 neatly mirrors the symbol. In our case the mechanism is more relaxed and it does not attempt to control individual lives. However, there is a clear sense in which media knowledge (or information) does control some of the ways in which we think about and assess the world. In the myriad events which daily pass across news editors' desks, selections are made according to whatever set of professional filters or intuitions are favoured by the newspaper or TV/radio station. The Western World's news media offer a limited number of these professional glosses or interpretive codes regardless of the nature of the information, clearly giving the impression of a world at one with itself, not a universe of threat, suspicion and disaster. Providers of new knowledge are notorious for their simplified, (melo) dramatic presentations on the one hand, and their partial 'self-censored' tendencies on the other. (Creators of Newspeak in the novel call this 'orthodoxy', i.e. not needing to think. 'Orthodoxy is unconsciousness'.)

One unusual media research project dramatically illustrates these points. Every year, 'Project Censored'[2], based in Northern California, selects 'the Top Ten Censored Stories' in the American news media. Nominations of important stories not featured by the main media are submitted to the Project from professionals, educators and members of the public. A panel, including Noam Chomsky and Jessica Mitford, then choose the top ten stories. Consistently, since 1974, the disjunction between actual media stories and 'censored' ones follows the lines etched by the attitude of mind which refuses to publish events which place national reputation at risk – the kind of events which suggest that holders of power might not always act decently, that they sometimes do things based upon sectional advantage, greed, and fear. In short, the media presents a world of events whose details depend, by and large, on knowledge which does not fracture the sense of concensus which power brokers must instil in populations in order to maintain the fictions of actions as once disinterested and for the general good. As a substitute, 'world knowledge' is touted which presents a fissiparous, uncontrolled out-there, an external drama in an infinite number of acts.

The following is a comparison of the ten biggest stories of 1982 as named by newspaper and broadcast member editors of Associated Press, compared with the stories given least coverage in 1982 as claimed by 'Project Censored'.

The Ten Biggest News Stories	*Top Ten Censored Stories*
1. The Nation's Economy.	1. Fradulent Safety Testing by large testing agency.
2. Cyanide-laced Tylenol.	2. Super-Secret Spy – surveillance on U.S. citizens.
3. Falklands War.	3. End of Equal Opportunity.
4. Death of Leonid Brezhnev.	4. Poisonous Agent White – pesticide.
5. Israel Invades Lebanon.	5. The Real Story of Central America.
6. Hinkley Jr. Found Innocent.	6. Reagan: America's Chief Censor.
7. Palestinian Camps Massacre.	7. U.S. Against the World – United States voting record in U.N.
8. First Artificial Heart Implant.	8. U.S. Firms traded with Nazis.
9. Washington Air Florida Crash.	9. $2 billion wasted on unnecessary use of fertiliser.
10. Football Strike.	10. Toxic wastes dumped on Indian lands.

The Associated Press List has seven death-related items and one event which caused widespread, if temporary, cultural disruption (No. 10), but may hardly be taken seriously as based on the criterion of 'newsworthiness'. The main point about the 'official' list is that most of the stories are powerfully dramatic and thrilling; they involve a sense of threat. Together, they represent a tableau of fear, a world 'out there' that might, if we relaxed, enter the near community. They are palpable warnings of the individual's insignificance, and siren calls for each of us to seek security. By contrast, the *Censored* list presents a 'near world' which needs to be confronted; whose actions scream out to be tested against something firmer and tougher than herd instinct. It is an uncomfortable list that requires the individual to ask questions, at least, about society, to replace timidity by scepticism and opposition.

If we read the Associated Press and the Censored lists as narratives they represent, respectively, 'goodthink' and 'crimethink'. And already, goodthinkers and crimethinkers are being created for the information-rich future. A recent report in *The Nation*[3] shows how America's major corporations have set out to make knowledge private. The Information Industry Association (whose members include IBM, Dow Jones, Lockheed, Xerox, Time Inc.) has made its primary goal 'to promote the development of private enterprise in the field of information and to gain recognition for information as a commercial product.' The Reagan administration has shown sympathy with such aims and public information agencies have been badly eroded. Information is well on the way to being controlled by market forces; and should demand prove slack for any type of information it would simply not be supplied. Control would be in the hands of a few powerful groups: a benign version of the Thought Police.

There is also a dramatic and disturbing resemblance to *Nineteen Eighty-Four* in another visual medium, the burgeoning video cassette movie industry. On the face of it, this is exactly the opposite to the novel, in that video machines offer the possibility for limitless variety based upon personal choice – as opposed to the restricted, official programming of Airstrip One. Further, videos give the individual control of images in the start/stop/freeze/re-wind mechanisms. Airstrip One has telescreen pictures that the individual cannot control in any way. However, at a deeper level there are strong resemblances, the most critical being the way in which leisure can be made *inert*.

In *Nineteen Eighty-Four* leisure activities are provided by and dominated by the State Tele–entertainment, sports, community hikes, savings campaigns and 'spontaneous demonstrations', the aim being to swamp the mind and supervise actions. Though such control does not happen at present, many of *our* leisure acts are 'supervised' in that the imagination is re-created for us, especially through television and video film. Video cassettes have invaded the leisure work of the mind because they give us the means to control space and time when endlessly replaying our favourite film (dream). The result is a creeping paralysis where the individual takes life from packaged fictions while his or her active leisure is confined to the hobby network. With the recent proliferation of specialist leisure magazines, the activity is further isolated, confined to the regular monthly reading and private practice. In short, the variety of options for the privatisation of leisure creates quietist situations with 'captive' populations energised communally only by the knowledge presented in media versions of the wider world: packaged isolation with the semblance of cultural freedom.

When we look at the production and distribution points, all appearance of variety fades. There, we find close-linked networks of industrial, cultural and military capital ensuring a centralisation of knowledge creation. A European example serves to make the point. Commercial television satellites are only a few years' distance from actuality, and the major European print publishing houses are preparing for the inevitable – with a little help from big business. At the end of 1980 France's aerospace giant Matra bought a controlling interest in Hachette, the country's leading publisher. The intention was to buy up writers and literary properties ready to service the demand for programmes which TV satellites will create. Matra is also a main contractor for the French Ariane rocket, which will launch the TV satellites.

One the military is involved in the production of culture, however indirectly, the world narrows, dissent is stifled; general notions of the nature of society are restricted to the few acceptable ones sanctioned by the holders of powerful information technology; and the rest of the friendly, connected world partakes of the fruits of the new technical wonders.

– 2 –

The Inner Party's greatest achievement in *Nineteen Eighty-Four* is the creation of a new language, Newspeak, designed actually to restrict the range of meaning and nuance – 'the only language in the world whose vocabulary gets smaller every year'. The rhetorical aim of Newspeak is to make 'other modes of thought impossible' and thereby bring about the 'good society' in which men and women will eventually become ducks and lay eggs in place of children. This new medium of expression (first newspeak, then duckspeak) will be accomplished by 'the invention of new words but chiefly by eliminating undesirable words and stripping such words as remained of unorthodox meanings and so far as possible of all secondary meanings whatever.'

Orwell divides words into three distinct classes: A, B and C vocabularies. The A vocabulary consists of homely words like *hit*, *run*, *dog*, *tree* needed for the business of everyday life. From these 'all ambiguities and shades of meaning' will be expunged. The B vocabulary contains words 'which have been deliberately constructed for political purposes: such words ... intended to impose a desirable mental attitude upon the person using them.' These are compound words, usually verbs combined with nouns, and in which the very process of compression is intended to expunge old meanings. Examples are 'bellyfeel', 'oldthink' or 'prolfeed', meaning 'the rubbishy entertainment and the spurious news' dished out by the Inner Party to the proles. The B vocabulary also has telescoped words, what we call acronyms today. Here is how Orwell explains this phenomenon:

'Even in the early decades of the twentieth century telescoped words and phrases had been one of the characteristic features of political language; and it had been noticed that the tendency to use abbreviations of this kind were marked in totalitarian countries and totalitarian organizations. Examples were such words as Nazi, Gestapo, Comintern, Inprecor, Agitprop. In the beginning the practice had been adopted as it were instinctively ..."[4]

These telescoped words are used quite consciously to narrow meaning and alter it. The C vocabulary is supplementary and consists entirely of scientific and technical terms.

What the Inner Party actually does, therefore, is to deprive people of their own words and in so doing, deprives them of memory. All words are stripped of secondary meanings so that very quickly memory, with its attendant richness and variety, atrophies; memories die when they go unrehearsed in words. More generally, the tactic is to obliterate history so that centres of opposition cannot grow, be they based upon ancestral memory or personal ideal. This rhetorical theory, however, is not developed in Oceania merely to prevent other ways of looking at the world; it is also a deliberate attempt to destroy feeling, to prevent connection, both mentally and emotionally. Mentally, Newspeak triumphs when people attain the gift of 'doublethink', where opposites are held simultaneously as 'truths' – War is Peace, Ignorance is Strength.

– 3 –

Newspeak in our time is the medium of expression for a tyrannical world view, whether in El Salvador, Cambodia or the United States Pentagon. Newspeak in our time is also 'mindset'. It provides a medium of expression for mental habits proper to people who believe 'in some process of feeling more efficient than the human soul.' The word mindset is often used to suggest a new computer mentality, but it is different from mind arrest. Orwell's Newspeak is mind arrest. Mindset is an ongoing phenomenon; it gets translated into policy.[5]

The President of the United States, for example, continues to call the Russians liars, cheats, and the 'focus of evil' in the world, but his mindset is worth billions of dollars. At NATO's defence ministers' meeting in Brussels, Reagan won support for a common Western defence strategy of pressing ahead on NATO deployment while pushing harder for arms control and peace.[6] How can we 'deploy' missiles (spread them around) and at the same time be pushing harder for arms control? It must be that war *is* peace, that deployment is employment, that missiles are meat. Consider this paragraph from the same magazine report:

'Reagan took up arms control again later in the week with retired General Edward Rouny, the chief US negotiator at the Geneva

START talks on long-range intercontinental missiles ... the General confirmed that Reagan was weighing a new START proposal that would conform with the recommendations of the Scowcraft commission which wants to improve overall ceilings on warheads rather than missiles. He also said that the administration was considering a Congressional proposal for a 'build down' offer which would allow the United States to modernize its nuclear arsenal while beginning to eliminate more outdated missiles.'[7]

A 'build down' to 'modernize' an arsenal? And START what? The acronym START stands for Strategic Arms Reduction Talks. START is the beginning of STOP, but who wants to stop arms production? Doublespeak. Doubletalk.

Acronyms are everywhere. ERA, IRA, SAM, AIDS? These cute-sounding names make injustice, revolution, missiles and disease seem innocuous. More than this, they suggest a never-never land of impenetrable mystery where people are infinitely busy but where nothing will ever get done. Finance[8], medicine and space exploration ... each has its own acronyms, but government and the military are the worst offenders. They seem unable to survive without abbreviations. Abbreviation is abstraction. Abstraction is also mindset. The way to escape living in the shadow of the bomb is to escape into space – outer and inner space – and each space has its jargon, jargon which gets translated into policy.

Mind arrest by the military deflates language because it causes people fear. But the mind arrest which religious cults practice is just as close in its world view to the world of *Nineteen Eighty-Four* for cults have in common with Winston's world a very palpable big brother, whether the Reverend Moon or the Reverend Jim Jones – who sent his flock to universal 'life' with cyanide poisoning. The Moonies and the followers of Jones must love the man or the icon, and in the name of love give up former ties, and then the memory of these former ties through the loss of the language, the words that carry memory. The experience of former Moonies testifies to the pressure of such love. A potential convert cannot go to the lavatory unless friends accompany him. There are also the long hours the convert is expected to labour in the 'vineyards of his lord', and the long hours he sustains on a diet of rice and vegetables. But what he receives in return is a 'god-centered life ... even though he is, as alleged, forcibly indoctrinated through hours of catechesis.'[9]

The longer one keeps hostages or converts and does not kill them but starves them and surrounds them by friends who feed them chants and slogans, the more likely it is that the hostages (converts) begin to consider the jailer or the organization powerful enough to be gods, for only gods can exercise the power of life or death, physical and spiritual. And hostages possessed of terror begin to speak in tongues of love. At first it is the cry of repentance, that you once belonged to a family of pigs, as in Patty Hearst's case. Recall the tapes released by the Simbionese Liberation Army. What we witness is several varieties of speaking in tongues ... language to arrest thought or language to put thought into action, but the direction is the same. The aim is power. Since there is no God in our world, anyone who takes hostages or hijacks a plane or kidnaps a child can play God and ask for love as well as submission. And hostages give it willingly. Orwell warned us about this 'syndrome'. The terrible, graphic final sections of the book and Winston's translation of O'Brien into God are the imagined forerunners of our own urban terrorism and of latter day spiritual messiahs.

Shirley Hazard sees it this way:

'Along with the transforming powers of technology and mass society there developed in the 19th century a sort of Industrial Revolution in human expression – an increasing tendency to renounce personal opinion in favor of generalized or official opinion and to evade self-knowledge and self-commitment through use of abstractions, a wish, in fact, to believe in some process of feeling more efficient than the human soul. There was also an associated new phenomenon of mass communication and mass advertising – that is of new words and usages not spontaneously but speciously brought into wide circulation as a means of profitably directing human impulse. (The word *jargon* incidentally derives from the twittering of geese).'[10]

The key word is *feeling*. Feeling other than violence is being destroyed; violence in itself is becoming a substitute for love, and we can trace the destruction of feeling on a world-wide scale to the brutalities of the holocaust. It is not alone that wars are cruel, that tyrants purge former friends, that juntas torture, that the PLO takes hostages or blows up department stores and synagogues. It is rather the terrible lack of connection. Living in a world, as Winston does, slowly going insane for the lack of connections, we are in danger of celebrating in ourselves Winston's final 'victory' when 'he loved Big Brother'.

What has this lack of connection to do with language in 1984? Newspeak in our time is language in defence of this lack of connection, with a decreasing awareness that any cruelty or barbarism we utter or make even needs defending. Our Newspeak is language without charity, lacking any connotation with human beings. Whether the language falls under A, B, or C according to Orwell's categories, the common denominator is the absence of life, the lack of connection or compassion, a running away from pain.

The Reagan administration has again given the A vocabulary a new twist. These are some samples from an article in *The Guardian*.[11]

'Being a responsible citizen in the Reagan era requires much more than simply salting away your tax cuts in a Swiss bank account or having your phone tapped. You must also learn to speak to administration officials in their native tongue. Here, for the truly responsible, are definitions of some of the most common terms in the language:

Death Penalty: A punishment that results in death. People who believe in death as punishment are called 'right-to-lifers'.

Disabled Worker: A leech who cuts off his leg so he can get a free ride from the government.

Domestic surveillance: A leisure service of the federal government whereby citizens are scrutinized to ascertain that their constitutional rights are not being violated.

Evolution: The now discredited theory that men are descended from apes. As we now know, it is not men, it is women who are descended from apes.

Peace: War.

Poor: An anachronism ... Today there are three economic classes in the US: 'the wealthy, the truly wealthy, and the not-so-wealthy. What used to be called the poor are the not-so-wealthy. The wealthy are the truly wealthy ...'

Senate: A legislative body charged by the Constitution with the important task of approving the President's programs.

Tree: A dangerous pollutant which emits deadly carbon dioxide into the air.'

One suspects that we are not too far from the real mind of Ronald Reagan. Big Buddy.

It is in the B vocabulary that we behold Newspeak 1984 flourishing in an unprecedented way. It is as if the military had memorised the Appendix to Orwell's book. Charles McCabe, late of the *San Francisco Chronicle*, devoted many of his daily columns to the problem of Newspeak, and during the Vietnam war he made it a practice to expose new words devised by the military. He called the words Pentagonese or Weasel Words. One of his columns begins: 'Have you noticed that the worse the fighting gets in Vietnam the sweeter, softer, and more emollient grows the official lingo used to describe the slaughter?'[12] And he reminded us that *escalate, police action, advisory intervention, expend ordnance* were a kind of 'mortician's lingo' to cover up death and savagery. He also reminded us how much we rely on acronyms or abbreviations to disguise: 'killed in action' (KIA) or 'dead on arrival' (DOA).

In another column called 'Nuclear Theology', McCabe described the men at the Pentagon as being so removed from reality that they were able to say things like: 'The problem of destruction is not fully solved'. Any wonder then that they could dream up euphemisms like 'taking out a city' to cover up 'the precise term for the total destruction of a city'? And terms like *controlled response, counter force, second strike* were all 'humane thermonuclear doctrine'. *Controlled response*, as nearly as McCabe could understand the term, meant that 'we refrain from the automatic bombing of cities in a nuclear war'.

After the military, these intellectual gymnastics are most easily acquired by politicians; and the Watergate episode provided us with abundant examples of linguistic perversions. One telling instance from the murky interlude in the American dream was a reported piece of doublethink, from the lips of Father John McLaughlin, Jesuit priest and 'special assistant' to President Nixon. The Father had previously been sent to South East Asia to defend Vietnam policy, including the bombing of North Vietnam and the mining of Haiphong Harbour, and according to *The New York Times* said:

'In evaluating the President's morality we ought to look at the extent to which he has produced a climate of charity in the international community at home. *He has reduced those forces* that would militate against charity, against constructive human interaction, and I would say to you that he has more than any other leader of this century reduced violence, aggression, insurgency, militarism and war in the twentieth century by a thousand per cent.'[13]

The cadences of a born-again rhetoric cannot hide the chilling resemblance to a polished, educated version of Duckspeak.

Both Watergate with its 'point in time' and Vietnam with its 'wasting' of civilian populations are behind us: but the imprint is fixed. We are beginning to internalise euphemisms as well as violence. The smashing successes of novels like Irving's *The World According to Garp* and *The White Hotel* by D. M. Thomas indicate that the artists among us are fighting this battle, not so much for the money as for the solace of getting it out of their systems. For the reality of our 1984 is power and violence, Orwell's vision of the totalitarian world before the ultimate revolution: 'If you want a picture of the future, imagine a boot stamping on a human face – for ever.' Cultural entrepreneurs in our 1984 have created that 'future' in their productions for leisure and information outlets. In 1982, *The New Yorker*'s 'Talk of the Town' column detailed over one 24-hour period the cultural and language surface of New York City.[14] The column detailed over 130 items, a representative selection of which appear below.

Newspaper Headlines
Slaying bares her secret life
Jean Harris weeps on TV as she relives murder night
Madman sears 2 with acid in subway
Job site protester shot in clash with hardhats
Kinky hubby's into bondage
Surrenders in cop's slaying
Citizens' gun use on rise in Houston
Detective shoots officer in argument in Queens

Movie Titles
First Blood   Alone in the Dark
Dawn of the Dead   The Burning
Funeral Home   Maniac
The Slumber Party Massacre   Horror Planet

Toys
Masters of the Universe: Skeletor Lord of Destruction
Masters of the Universe: Zodiac Cosmic Enforcer
GI Joe a Real American Hero
Mobile Missile System (MSS) with Removable Missiles you elevate
and swivel

Games   Combat Rock
Stay Alive   Paranoid
Survival   Back to the Bone
Conspiracy
Curse of the Cobras   *Television Films*
                                     Roots of Evil
Video Games   Hear no Evil
Communist Mutants from Space   Peeping Tom
Night Stalker   Murder on Lenox Avenue
Gangster Alley   An Eye for an Eye
Rip Off   Destroyer
Berzerk   The Howling
Demon Attack
Bomb Squad   *Rock Groups*
                                     Cheap Trick
Records   Missing Persons
Screaming for Vengeance   The Clash
Children of the Grave   The Destroyers

That is why we must pause in our reading of *Nineteen Eighty-Four* to examine language, the language of our television shows, the language of advertising, the language of Pentagonese. That is why we must pause to examine the sounds and the words of Acid and Punk Rock, the very names of the groups, to examine even the language of Atari games, to behold the language of thud, language sometimes encased in velvet gloves, but language nonetheless of men who are beginning to play at God in the sense that Big Brother is God – not a god that brings life to people but the god that brings death. It is being achieved by the widespread substitution of old cultural metaphors which clustered around abstractions like decency, charity, compassion, tenderness by metaphors of the machine, whose cybernetic clatter numbs the collective imagination and silences the old meanings and dims the memories which gave a human shape to experience. That sentence is a version of Winston's anguish and the partial fulfilment of Orwell's warning.

Chapter 6

Christopher Roper
Taming the Universal Machine

In the years since *1984* was first published, computers have often been seen as harbingers of an Orwellian world of total surveillance and thought control. It would be almost unthinkable not to include them in a retrospective consideration of his book and its place in the future. Yet in most important respects George Orwell was far from prophetic. He did not understand the new forms of social control and manipulation which computers would make possible, and there is no indication in any of his books that he was the slightest bit interested in computers or other aspects of information technology.

Even though the first electronic computers were being built as Orwell wrote, his model of repression did not depend on new technologies. His novel-writing machine was clearly a mechanical gadget requiring spanners and oil cans; Winston Smith received his messages down a pneumatic tube like the ones which used to deliver change in department stores; and the citizens of Oceania were more likely to fall into the hands of the Thought Police as a result of betrayal by an informer than from being spotted through the telescreen. Nevertheless, there is something Orwellian about the passivity of the British population today in the face of adverse social and economic developments, which are fatalistically accepted as the working out of immutable natural laws.

The most striking high-tech feature of life in Orwell's *1984* is the all-seeing telescreen, although he is not concerned with the workings of such a device. He does not explain how a gymnastics instructor, presumably supervising millions of Oceanians at their morning exercises, could spot the fact that one of them, Winston Smith, was not doing his best. The telescreen could have been presented as some kind of cybernetic device, automatically monitoring the population for deviant behaviour and then feeding back the appropriate rebuke. But this would have been a highly novel idea in 1948, and there is no hint that Orwell's mind was moving in that direction. In fact, 1948 also saw the publication of Norbert Wiener's influential book *Cybernetics*, which sparked discussions leading in a rather different direction from that pointed by Orwell. But the telescreen is largely a metaphor for depersonalised Stalinism and Fascism, in which the

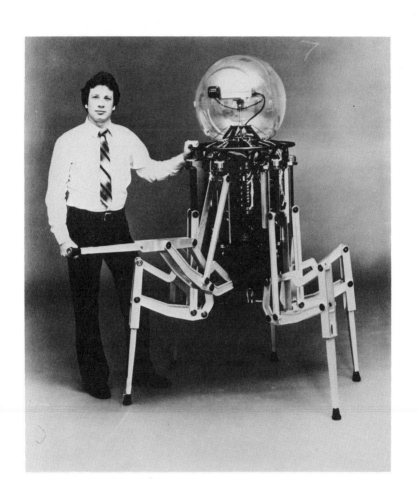

State ends all vestiges of privacy by finally being able to look into a citizen's home.

At the same time, an understanding of the place of computers in the modern world provides elements for an analysis of why Orwell was mistaken. It may also help us to understand the crisis of democratic politics in this and other advanced industrialised countries. I shall argue that the main effects of computers on our society have been:

- to reduce the cost of commercial and bureaucratic transactions, permitting a segmentation of markets, and a previously unimaginable expansion of consumerism.
- to reduce the need for a great deal of active surveillance by improving mechanisms of passive surveillance.
- to elevate an apparent freedom of choice to the forefront of Capitalist ideology.
- to decentralise work, strengthening community politics at the expense of workplace politics.
- to end the age of broadcasting. Narrowcasting and interactive networks will have replaced broadcasting as the dominant media by the end of the century.
- to create an information overload, which has not yet been assimilated by our culture except through a process of devaluation and trivialisation.

When Orwell wrote, information technology was not even a concept, let alone a phrase, and Orwell would surely have cast it into the nether circles of Newspeak. But there was, we might now say, a technology of information. This consisted of printed books, magazines and newspapers; still photography, films, radio and (embryonically) television; gramophones and (embryonically) tape recorders; telex and the telephone. Electromechanical accounting and data processing machines, digital computers, satellite telecommunications, video recorders and photocopiers were all hardly imaginable.

The first computers were forbidding machines. To start with, their utterances were clearly written in Newspeak. Ugly and meaningless acronyms and abbreviations were sprayed across electricity bills and rate demands in illegible upper case script. Secondly, they were unbelievably crude in their transactions with ordinary human beings. Since the data was fed in through punched cards prepared by bored and overworked operators, it was almost impossible to track down errors. The computers returned time and again to the original mistake. Guarded and served by data processing departments in specially controlled atmospheres, no ordinary person ever came into direct contact with a computer, and they represented impersonal, uncaring bureaucracy at its worst. Some of their more imaginative inventors even claimed that these universal machines were universal brains, which could threaten human supremacy. And all the while they were presented by officialdom as a great blessing to humanity. It was easy to believe that an entity as crass as Big Brother lived in the entrails of such machines.

Many people have not updated their view of computer capabilities and do not realise the extent to which most commercial and bureaucratic transactions are now, fairly painlessly, computerised. Furthermore, a modern personal computer is no more mysterious or difficult to operate than a car. Seen from the vantage point of 1983, Orwell's Oceania is technologically primitive. The speakwrite is perhaps the only believable gadget, and it seems to be a fairly innocent piece of equipment, a word-processor which converts speech to print. They will be on the market shortly. It is already possible to buy an attachment to a microcomputer which converts typed input into synthesized speech.

Passive Intelligence Gathering

In order to discuss information technology in terms of the novel, one must first understand the ways in which post-war history in the OECD countries has diverged from Orwell's apocalyptic vision. The most striking difference concerns the nature of social control. Citizens of Oceania feared the telescreen because they never knew when the Thought Police might switch in to their particular monitor. But this was still *active* surveillance, little different in kind from traditional telephone tapping, or the kind of police spying which was so pervasive in Stalinist Russia. In reality, computers excel in *passive* surveillance, alerting the controlling authority to any deviation from an expectable pattern: the household which makes too many international telephone calls, or uses an abnormal amount of electricity; the individual who makes too many unexplained journeys to Libya or Zurich; the telephone conversation mentioning names of individuals of interest to the authorities; unusual traffic patterns in a particular neighbourhood; or credit card holders making particular kinds of regular purchase. This is the new element introduced by the computer, and this possibility of monitoring large populations for potentially deviant behaviour will become even easier through the use of 'artificial' intelligence techniques. These involve the computer working almost autonomously, and enable investigators to discover behaviour patterns that they were not specifically seeking.

Computers are routinely used for the passive collection of this type of intelligence, which should reduce the need for a great deal of active surveillance. If one accepts the right of a society to impose repressive laws to protect itself from burglary, murder, rape or armed conspiracies to overthrow the established order, then passive surveillance may be more acceptable than active surveillance with police on the streets, and secret police in the background. The real question is how we make the rules; who controls the surveillance; whether the rules are publicly declared and understood by the whole population.

In general, computers have made the impositions of state bureaucracies *less* burdensome, and the more backward a country in relation to information technology, the more oppressive its bureaucracy is likely to be. Advanced information technology does not seem to make it any more or less likely that a state will actively supervise every detail of its citizens' lives or violate their elementary human rights. Argentina's military authorities, for example, made extensive use of computerised surveillance techniques in the repression of 1976–79, and afterwards exporting them to Central America, where electricity and telephone bills were monitored to discover safe houses kept by guerrillas in Guatemala City. But the Argentine repression was not quantitatively or qualitatively different from other, less technically refined reigns of terror, in Indonesia in 1966, Chile in 1973, Kampuchea in 1977–8, Nicaragua in 1978, or El Salvador in 1981–2. Once individuals have been identified as targets for active surveillance, computers facilitate the task.

European and North American security forces, too, use computerised surveillance to counter clandestine groups such as the Red Army Faction in Germany and the Weather Underground in the United States. But states have always mobilised all their resources against such groups, and it is striking how ineffective the police of those countries were, with all their sophisticated equipment, in picking up their sworn enemies. Hundreds of wanted 'terrorists' are still at large, and the major breakthroughs have come as a result of old-fashioned police work, and betrayals – probably under old-fashioned torture – by those who have been captured. Neither reigns of terror nor intensive manhunts are products of the computer age.

What is new, in Britain, the United States or any other advanced industrialised state, is that we exist as numbers and ciphers in computers belonging to government departments, banks and other commercial enterprises. Some people object to such computerised personal documentation on the grounds that it increases the potential control which could be exercised by some future repressive government. This is rather like the argument of the National Rifle Association in the United States, which objects to the registration of guns because the existence of central records would permit an invading Communist army to 'disarm the American People'. In fact, the new technology should make it easier for us to exercise political control over the uses to which the information is put. Cardboard files with handwritten notes are extraordinarily inaccessible to anyone but the immediate bureaucracy which created them.

Computers also played a central, as yet unquantified, role in reducing the unit cost of most paper transactions in the period 1950 to 1980, and in producing the unprecedented economic growth of the OECD economies during those years. These savings applied as much to bureaucratic transactions as to commercial exchanges. And although the middle classes hated receiving their bank statements in the form of a computer printout, instead of written out in the crabbed hand of a servile bank clerk, the main beneficiaries of computerised hire purchase and credit cards, if beneficiary is the right word, were the skilled workers and white collar workers, who did not previously have ready access to bank overdrafts. In these sectors, house and car ownership expanded rapidly after the Second World War; holidays abroad became commonplace. And few of those whose life styles changed as a result of the consumer boom of the past 30 years would vote for a return to a high cost computerless world.

The hidden cost of electronic transactions is the audit trail we each leave behind us, from birth to death, each and every time we give our name and address. George Orwell saw only the surveillance, the crude official lies, and the growth of a totalitarian state. He did not foresee that the pill would be coated in sugar, or that obesity would be a greater problem than malnutrition in Oceania. Despite all the legislation which might be passed to protect us from misuse of our electronic trail, it is an inescapable part of the consumer society. You cannot have the one without the other.

Orwell was also wrong in suggesting that the succeeding 35 years might see a shrinking of public access to culture and knowledge. Winston Smith was even confused as to the date; thanks to our digitized time-pieces, we don't just know the date, we know the time to the nearest tenth of a second. There has equally been an explosion of accessible knowledge through books, radio and television. Where official information is concerned the photocopier has provided an important extension of public access to official secrets. It is certainly arguable that the Freedom of Information Act in the United States was a direct result of the impossibility of making Washington leak-proof. If Richard Nixon had been unable to record his own conversations, it is unlikely that the Watergate scandal would ever have threatened his tenure of the Presidency.

The problem, in our neck of Oceania at least, is not the lack of information, but the lack of any simple way of sorting or evaluating the flow of indigestible and undigested facts. Of course, the facts are mixed with a generous helping of misinformation, fantasy and downright lies. Other information is deliberately concealed from us. But the Left has discovered to its cost that the great problem is not so much acquiring information to make its case, as to persuade people to listen, take note, and take action.

It is a dangerous illusion of the British Left, and more particularly of left-wing journalists, that if only the British people were told the facts, Jerusalem would be right round the corner. It simply isn't true, and it doesn't do to simply blame censorship or computers for our failures to communicate our views to the traditional constituency of the Left. Most of the techniques of propaganda through news management either preceded the new technology, or do not depend upon it. The main effect of the computer and other technological advances has simply been to swell the flood of printed and stored information.

These observations are not intended as criticisms of the book. Orwell was not interested in technological prophecy, and *1984* has sharp and immediate relevance in countries like Argentina, where governments are not so very different from the totalitarianism he described. *1984* is based on his experiences of Communism and Fascism in the 1930s and 40s, set in the deprived landscape of post-war Britain. It is not a very helpful text for the analysis of the political impact of electronic media in Western Europe or North America today.

Dictatorship of the Consumer?

A rather different starting point would be to locate information technology in the political economy of 1983, charting some of the changes which have taken place over the past 30 years. The greatest change has been the consumer boom, affecting all questions of taste and fashion, and mediated for most people through television and popular music. The implied message of the broadcast media is that we all have virtually unlimited choices of lifestyle. And although we all know that economic and social reality substantially reduces the range, there is just enough reality behind the Bingo-style promises of the consumer society to keep most of us living within the limits of social acceptability. Even though competition among the leading corporations may not be particularly significant, adjustment to changing public tastes, and attempts to manipulate public taste, are critical to their profitability.

In general, the public sector has been far slower than private capital to recognise the political potential of illusory choice as a political slogan. The Conservatives may make a parade of their devotion to the principle of consumer choice. But even under a Conservative government, the public sector instinctively offers standard services and standard products, and relies on coercion rather than blandishment to ensure public acceptance. The idea that government departments should tailor their services to public demand seems shocking to most civil servants.

This is a hang-over from a period when there were more important economies of scale in producing a standard product than there are today. When the modern state took shape in the nineteenth century, the private sector, too, offered limited choices, and monopolies were coercive rather than seductive. Choice was a luxury, available to a relatively small leisured class. Information technology has made it economically possible to respond to a wide variety of demands, and to predict the likely demand for a given service. Desire for choice has become a permanent feature of the British political landscape.

If socialists now wish to restore enthusiasm for nationalised industries, and a strengthened role for the social services, they will have to demonstrate commitment to the idea of consumer choice, and also control. This would require a degree of decentralisation, and confrontations with bureaucratic and sectional interests, which currently provide the core of institutional support for the Labour Party. It is not enough to say that the choices offered by Mrs Thatcher are largely illusory, or that it is easier to take responsibility for one's own welfare if one has inherited a family company like Mr Thatcher. It's true, but it does not meet the point. Interestingly enough, the Hungarians, in the most computer-literate nation in Eastern Europe, are seeking ways of introducing consumer choice, and of decentralising control of the economy through private enterprise, cooperatives, and free markets.

In the absence of some new direction, not provided by the Labour governments of 1964–70 or 1974–79, Britain is going to move further towards the Thatcherite ideal of an atomised society of competing individuals who will have chosen to reject the collectivist ideas of the Labour Party. The new political economy will be mediated through the new technology, through centralised access, at home, to a mixture of entertainment and advertisements. This is likely to lead to a more important transformation of the public sector than any number of nationalisations or denationalisations. It is a far cry from Big Brother, but nonetheless unsettling.

Social control would depend on shaping and mobilising taste and opinion through the market place, around a consensus of consumers, whose behaviour will have become utterly predictable through the application of statistical analysis to the daily choices we make: to watch television, visit the pub, to withdraw our funds from that bank, to support that football team, or to visit Paris. In addition, public opinion polls and other market surveys will continue to advance in scope and accuracy. That's democracy, some may cry, and Butlins is certainly a better model for the future than the Gulag Archipelago. The idea of automatic rule through the sum of consumer decisions is a nightmare for most of us, even when our own right to choose an alternative solution is recognised.

One way in which Left intellectuals escape from this dilemma is to blame the media. If only, they wail, the press and television were not controlled by the Tories, our message would get through, and everything would be different. This is actually as spurious as the notion that if only the people were informed they would think differently. In fact, the problem is that the Left regards the idea of promoting or selling its ideas to be immoral. The idea that they should tailor their policies to public opinion is not far short of betrayal. For while Thatcher has extended the scope of the Tories' ideological readjustment, the Labour Party has, if anything, regressed towards a more centralised model of society.

The Information Revolution

This is likely to be a doomed enterprise, as another important consequence of information technology, again not foreseen by George Orwell, is the decentralisation of work. To be fair to Orwell, his contemporaries, the inventors of digital computers, men like Alan Turing or John Von Neumann, did not foresee the social consequences of their inventions. They did not expect that computers would threaten to replace typewriters within 35 years. Turing believed in 1950 that it would be 70 years before a computer could play a game of chess well enough to beat a chess master. That point was actually reached in less than 30 years. Today, computers communicating with computers make it possible to manage global corporations on a highly centralised basis, or to locate service departments in cheaper office space, away from the main office, and close to the homes of cheap women workers. Some classes of information work can be done on a micro-computer or terminal at home.

This transformation contains potential for both good and bad. It can lead to the exploitation of homeworkers, or offer the chance of useful work to people who are too severely disabled to leave their homes. But the Labour Party can scarcely be blind to the demographic changes being brought about by this decentralisation of work; the dispersion of the population from the inner cities into suburban areas; the increasing importance of the car and the lorry at the expense of buses and trains; and the collapse of old industries. For good and ill, computers strike at existing patterns of work, weaken the unions, and increase the power of managers. They may ultimately lead to a strengthening of the local community, rather than the workplace, as a focus of political life.

Technological changes are also likely to accelerate rapidly over the next five years, and important innovations will include:

1. Microcomputers will increase in power and versatility. They will have more built-in memory, and will be easily linked to the outside world through the television set or telephone lines.
2. Video disc and tape recorders, controlled by microcomputers, will arrive faster than cable television to widen the choice for home entertainment and education. Video discs, in particular, offer cheap mass storage for the home computer user.
3. Microcomputers will be easier to use, with standard architectures, a great deal of built-in software, and high resolution screens, mixing text and graphics at will.
4. Electronic cash transfers for shop purchases will become as routine as the automatic cash dispensers in banks. You will be able to debit your account directly through a terminal in the shop.

At the same time, new markets will come into being, based on new ways of using microcomputers. Just as word processing was an unexpected use for a computer (not foreseen by IBM for example), so there will be other surprises. One emerging phenomenon in the United States is the development of open networks, into which anyone can plug, and computer bulletin boards catering for people who send messages to one another via microcomputers, acoustic couplers and the telephone system. This allows for a sharing of information among research networks and pressure groups, or coordination of political activity around the country, far more effectively than would be possible by mail or telephone. American universities have become centres of a computer culture, which is far more complex and rich than anything which yet exists in Britain. The models are still limited and relatively expensive but they do point to changes as pervasive as those introduced by the telephone, radio or television.

Unless the British Left finds ways of reacting positively to the changed environment, Labour could effectively be excluded from power for a generation, not because the new media will be used to pipe overt Tory propaganda into the home, but because the new media will offer CHOICE and diversity, which happens also to be the slogan of the Conservative Party.

One option is certainly to reject the whole notion of new technology, or to accept it so grudgingly as to amount to rejection. This has been the general posture of the Labour movement, and there are good historical reasons why they have adopted blocking tactics. The problem is that their defensive tactics have failed. They have not protected the union members from job losses, prevented industries from collapsing, or won the loyalty and trust of the working population. The alternative is to find some new model of work which will permit a transition to general acceptance and use of computers. One should not underestimate the size of this problem. For the transformations now taking place are sufficiently dramatic to allow us to talk about an Information Revolution, which, like its industrial precursor, imposes new ways of working, destroying many jobs, and creating others, shifting power and influence into new hands.

The Struggle for Control

There have been, and will continue to be, a series of struggles to appropriate the electronic media. These play such a critical part in determining patterns of taste and policy as to make them a principal focus of political struggle. The contenders are:

- Monopolist commercial interests, which have controlled radio and television broadcasting in the United States for the past 50 years;
- Central governments, which controlled broadcasting in its first phases in Britain, but had to give way to commercial interests.
- Decentralised, community-controlled groups, typified by subscriber-supported radio stations in the United States, or university radio stations in Latin America.

This third possibility has provided a focus for the dreams of many liberal and libertarian thinkers. In no country in the world, however, have such interests been strong enough to win more than limited access to the airwaves. Special interest broadcasting in the United States by educational and religious groups comes closest to the ideal, although a night of watching open access television in New York is enough to drive you back to the safe consensus of the BBC.

The most important new element introduced to information

technology by the computer, however, is not simply variety, but interactivity. All previous media, from storytellers to television, have been unidirectional, transmitting the ideas of the originator/author to an audience. The audience could choose to read/listen/watch or not, and could request changes in the programme, which might or might not be granted. But a person on the receiving end could not choose between variant endings to a film or book, build his/her own cartoon films from a library of animated sequences, or ask for more information about a poorly understood item on the news. Such interaction was impossible because it would have affected all members of the audience. Computers are making this kind of customising possible. It is not available yet, but the principle of a user controlling the inflow of information, in as wide a range of fields as I have indicated, with a wide variety of options, is technically quite possible, and has been achieved experimentally in several restricted environments.

George Orwell thought in terms of unidirectional media. The telescreen was bidirectional but only in the sense that it allowed the central controller to observe the viewers. It did not permit them to feed their inputs back into the system, or to communicate with one another. In the Ministry of Truth, history was constantly being rewritten, but this was done centrally, not by the consumers of the news. In the world I see coming into being, there will be many versions of historical truth, created in the form of a mosaic by the many actors, linked in an electronic network, widely accessible to people who will add their own testimony, their own criticisms, and their own embellishments. Ideally it should give us back some of the control over our own history which we lost when we began to move from an essentially oral culture towards an essentially written culture several thousand years ago.

People may think it unlikely that anything of this kind could happen without the goodwill of central governments or monopoly capital. But means of communication themselves have political weight, and may ultimately determine the kind of governments we have. The expansion of consumer choice may permit new forms of interaction. These could give us back the kind of political and cultural life, which, at another level, the reconstruction of democracy around the principle of consumer choice, seems to threaten. Furthermore, the Thatcherite ideal of individuals taking responsibility for their lives could be subverted by the notion of communities of individuals collectively taking responsibility for their own affairs – and challenging Thatcherism on its own terms.

Interactive media will continue the transformation of society begun by radio and television. We are already beginning to see 'narrowcasting' replacing broadcasting, with radio and television programmes designed for relatively small segments of the population. The Open University is perhaps the most advanced use of narrowcasting in this country. But whilst narrowcast media are characterised by a high degree of reader/audience participation, the next generation of truly interactive media will take this process a stage further.

It will depend on large-scale wiring of homes and offices, creating multiple networks of microcomputers, mainframe computers, and video libraries, permitting the transformation of digital data into images on a screen, or sound, as well as printed messages. In such a network, the role of author/narrowcaster would be blurred with that of participant/consumer/user, as many different people would be making their inputs to a collectively shared output.

The main obstacles to such a development are financial, political and cultural, not technical. It is still expensive and unfamiliar terrain, and it threatens many entrenched interests across the political spectrum. Developments in the United States in the field of personal computer networking suggest that it will come. There will be a delay, similar to the one which intervened between the spread of CB Radio in the United States and over here. But there has not been a single mass cultural development in the United States which has not crossed the Atlantic in this century, and there is no reason to suppose that personal computing is going to be any different. In fact, the British Telecom monopoly is already being broken up to make way for the new media.

The cultural obstacle to such a major shift in our use of media is that we would not know what to do with such a facility. We are not prepared by any previous experience to participate in an electronic message system to exchange information and ideas. Likely early uses will be as banal as those associated with CB Radio (avoiding speed traps; setting up sexual encounters with strangers; and discussing the minutiae of the medium itself). But this should not be allowed to obscure the possibilities of the new media to subvert the deeper and nastier consequences of our new political economy. The poverty of the present technology is no reason for not participating. There is an urgent need for experiments which are not sponsored by the government or big business, which are culturally autonomous, and which aim at community appropriation of the new media. The political questions posed by Orwell remain valid today. Are we to become simply the twitching synapses of a state system which we neither understand nor control? Or can the potential transformation of our collective nervous system actually liberate us?

The intellectual parents of information technology, contemporaries of George Orwell, like the intellectual parents of nuclear weaponry, were, in many cases, liberal intellectuals, victims of Fascism, and subsequently of McCarthyism. The world took their insights and discoveries and put them to its own multifarious purposes. These material consequences of abstract speculations have changed the global predicament and opportunity in ways which were not foreseen by Orwell or anyone else. Many of those living now, forced to make changes for which they were not prepared, may wish the 'universal machine' had never been conceived. Some of them will try to live out their lives without facing the new choices and the new dilemmas. But that option is not open to most of the human race. We are going to have to find ways of living with instant feedback, knowing that our lives are open to scrutiny, and that the lives of others are open to us. This will require new political and social conventions, new ways of being.

Chapter 7

Mike Cooley and Mike Johnson
The Robots' Return?

Had George Orwell sought to describe the means of production compatible with his *Nineteen Eighty-Four* he could hardly have done better than the design of the industrial systems planners. Mechanisation of the modern factory has come to be symbolised by the industrial robot – a machine designed to make certain processes more efficient and to replace the production worker. Yet the direct work of making or assembling a product is not where mechanisation is now likely to have the greatest effect. For the scope and mode of mechanisation has been enhanced by systems planning to the point where the *overall* process of design, manufacture and management are at once controlled by a centralised computer processing system. The central core of modern production, as Orwell's *Nineteen Eighty-Four* laments, is thus the contradiction between human autonomy and the traditional hierarchical structures of organisation. But is it possible that the academic model of autonomy and reflective thought could be re-directing technology in the spheres of industry, commerce and government? Or is the reverse true, that the factory model is spreading via computer mechanisation to the research laboratories, centres of education and decision-making?

Those concerned with the cultural, political and social development of society, as Orwell was, view with increasing alarm the fanatical missionary zeal of the computocrats. Armed with a childlike, boy scout optimism about technology, these industrial Eichmanns ('I only did what I was told') blindly supercharge the vehicle of technological change on its exponential way, remarkably oblivious to the consequences of their work. They ensure that anything that can possibly be computerised will be computerised. They are, as Joseph Weitzenbaum, Professor of Computer Science at the Massachusetts Institute of Technology, succinctly put it, 'Like children with a hammer. They view the whole world as a nail'.[1]

History is for the systems planners something you repeat rather than learn from. Thus they are quite happily beginning to repeat in the field of white collar intellectual conceptual work, and in the so-called 'new' jobs, most of the mistakes we already made at such enormous cost at earlier historical points when skilled manual work was subjected to technological change. Moreover, because they have a limited historical view it seems natural for them to assume that scientific and technological progress is an absolute societal advance. For the computercrats, the historical accretion of any knowledge and experience that is not defined in 'scientific' discourse or empirically observable in economic terms – that experience of the working environment, whether at home or in the workplace – is entirely neglected. For them computerisation is part of technological progress and technological progress is by definition 'good'. The nature and form of that progress and alternative forms of progress are not matters open to discussion.

If really pressed to justify what they are doing they will assert that automation, computerisation and the use of robotic equipment will free human beings from soul-destroying, routine, back-breaking tasks and leave them free to engage in more creative work. The systems, they suggest, will lead to a shorter working week, longer holidays and more leisure time. Pressed further, they may add as a sort of occupational bonus that the mass of data made available to us through information retrieval systems will mean that the decisions we make will be much more logical, creative and scientific.

At the centre of this argument is a powerful conception of science as the means to create a future society unbelievably rich, leisured, orderly and efficient. But to argue thus is to ignore the growing chasm between that which technology could provide (its potential) and that which it actually does provide (its reality). That reality is structured by in-built design assumptions which reflect a series of value systems, predominantly those of the white, male, capitalist, warrior hero. They also tend to be value systems in which human judgement is regarded as at best erratic and at worst, dangerous. Orwell himself, in the extract from the Goldstein book, and in accordance with the principles of 'double think', described the inevitable gap between scientific potential and reality:

'The dangers inherent in the machine are still there. From the moment when the machine first made its appearance it was clear to all thinking people that the need for human drudgery, and therefore to a great extent for human inequality, had disappeared. If the machine were deliberately used to that end, hunger, overwork, dirt, illiteracy and disease could be eliminated within a few generations ...'[2]

In practice any real shift in resources in that direction would challenge the hierarchical relations of his futurist society. Hence for Orwell technology, and further patterns of thought and enquiry that could give rise to new inventions, were strictly directed in support of the existing order and its war machine.

Computocrats on the Shop Floor

Today the typical factory relies on a great variety of machines, and factory work is widely supposed to consist largely of tending machines. New developments in relations between humans and machines also tend to be viewed primarily in the context of production, and manufacturing in particular. This approach also places most emphasis on the social implications of mechanisation – as the introduction of machines has affected particular jobs, conditions and skills. There is an irony here. For production in the 'workerless factory' or the 'automated office' is in fact dependent on the mechanisation of intellectual conceptual work in the higher echelons of industry, commerce and the scientific establishment. What is really involved is re-designing the product and controlling productivity at a level far removed from actual 'production'.

The major challenge for the captains of industry, and the major opportunity for increased productivity, is therefore the organising, scheduling and managing of the *total* manufacturing enterprise, from design to fabrication, distribution and field service. The productivity of the factory worker depends to a large extent on the design of the product and on the way the resources of labour, raw materials and machines are brought together. Without improvement in these functions it is not clear that even a total replacement of shop floor workers by robots would have much effect on the total output of the factory. For this reason the important contribution to the productivity of the factory offered by new systems-designed technology is in its capacity to link design, management and manufacturing.

Manufacturing includes a vast array of activities and enterprises, and those that design and manufacture 'discrete' products, rather than merely process raw materials, are a broad and varied category. They encompass the fabrication and assembly of motor vehicles, aircraft, computers, furniture, appliances, foods, clothing, packing, building materials and machine tools. And it is in these industries that the application of systems planning is most pronounced. At first, manufacturers introduced new technologies to the shop floor on a piecemeal basis, particularly crude methods of programming such as the numerical control of machine operations. These widely adopted systems are totally dehumanising, reducing skilled work to tedium, and a recent report in the *American Machinist* suggested that the ideal workers for them would be the mentally retarded. The author advocated a mental age of 12.[3]

Ironically, the design of these technologies is rooted in the so-called 'natural' sciences. Within this discipline we do not regard something as scientific unless it displays three predominant char-

acteristics – predictability, repeatability and mathematical quanti-
fiability. These by definition preclude human judgement, intuition
and subjectivity. It is a process which inevitably puts production
before the producer, the objective before the subjective, the
quantitative before the qualitative, creating a situation in which the
human being is controlled by the machine rather than the other way
round. To quote Marx:

'As machinery, the instrument of labour assumes a material mode of
existence which necessitates the replacement of human force by
natural forces, and the replacement of the rule of thumb by the
conscious application of natural science. In manufacture the
organisation of the social labour process is purely subjective: it is a
combination of specialised workers. Largescale industry, on the
other hand, possesses in the machine system an entirely objective
organisation of production, which confronts the worker as a pre-
existing material condition of production.'[4]

In the mid-1960s, however, a new development occurred. Engineers
from General Motors began to work with programming specialists at
IBM to develop a system for Computer-Aided Design (CAD).
Traditionally, the machinist set up the machine according to
drawings supplied by the designer; and when numerically controlled
machine tools were introduced, the programmer who prepared the
sequence of instructions still obtained the information from
drawings. Designers and engineers both soon recognised, however,
that CAD could be used to obtain the geometrical detail direct from a
data base, thus eliminating the drawing entirely. Information in
design work and programming machine functions are also available
in a similar way through computerisation.

The computocrats claim that the application of CAD improves
productivity in the drawing room; that it also improves accessibility
of the design throughout the company; and that it increases savings in
planning and the identification of parts during assembly, and so on.
This may be so, but in as much as the design process is pre-conceived
in a narrow conception of *reality*, the measurement of benefit is
exclusive and tautologous. As Weizenbaum put it: 'For technocrats,
all problems are technical problems which must have technical
solutions'.[5] A purely technical ascription of production leaves what
Marx called the 'material mode of existence' without social form.
Once alien and objective criteria are introduced into all areas of
manufacturing – in the guise of externally controlled machines – the
worker is not only deskilled physically, he (or she) is also rendered
mute and lifeless; production itself ceases to have any real and
humanly sustainable purpose. In effect, work is abolished because

social engagement and self-defined conceptions of the world as it is experienced appear only on the margin of a computerised 'workerless factory system'.

The Swedish researcher Sandberg has pointed out how the 'conceptualisation and planning of work on a day to day basis, even on a second to second basis, is being taken away from the immediate producers and concentrated in the departments of planning'.[6] Even where a small space is left for decision-making by the worker, this is still paced and controlled by the machine. In the case of word processing, one technical director told a recent conference in London: 'Your secretaries will be required to be more productive; there will be no more walking, talking, thinking or dreaming'. He went on to point out that given suitable sub-routines one could count the frequency with which the 'delete' button is pressed and hence provide the secretary with an 'error profile' at the end of each day. It would be equally possible to monitor the frequency at which the keys are depressed so that an 'activity profile' for the typist's day is made possible. In both cases, this represents the increasing control and 'pacing' of manual work.

It should be borne in mind, however, that precisely the same sort of development is taking place at the highest levels of intellectual work. The desire to Taylorise intellectual work is of course of long standing, and the father of the computer industry, Charles Babidge, in his *Economy of Machinery and Manufacturers*, anticipated Taylorism in the field of intellectual work when he wrote: 'We have already mentioned what may perhaps appear paradoxical to some of our readers, that the division of labour can be applied with equal success to mental work as well as mechanical operations and that it ensures in both the same economy of time'.

The application of computers to appraise and quantify intellectual work is a trend that must be seriously considered. Whereas human desires, feelings and subjective judgements are parts of any creative mental activity, they remain beyond scientific evaluation. A number of 'scientific' studies display a Platonic view of the world of understanding. Historically, such intellectual reason has been held to be superior to forms of knowledge based on experience. However, the social content of such views has always depended on class or caste hierarchies. Knowledge, whether 'scientific' or not, becomes a reactionary force in the service of an elite unless it is capable of freely progressing in real social terms.

In 1974, a paper in the journal *Work Study* entitled 'The Classification and Terminology of Mental Work' suggested that much progress had already been made in this direction.[7] The paper discusses in detail how management can now classify input, output and processing movements; and how these can be subdivided down into basic mental operations. It even goes so far as to draw a distinction between active and passive modes of *cognition*: the passive reception of visual signals/seeing is ranked below looking, or its active version. And on the same model hearing is graded into hearing and listening. The paper implies that these techniques will be used in the more clerical aspects of mental work. It concludes: 'We have tried to show that mental work is a valid and practical field of work study, that the basic mental motions exist and can be classified in a meaningful way provided that one does not trespass too far into the more complex mental routines and processes. A set of basic mental motions can be identified, named, described and coded as a basis for future human research leading to the compilation of standard times. There is a good prospect that such times can play a valuable part in work study'. General Motors' psychologist Howard Carlson has pointed out that 'the computer may be to middle management what the assembly line is to the hourly worker', and evidence abounds that intellectual workers at many levels are now being increasingly controlled and proletarianised by the systems they themselves have helped to evolve.

Academic Factories

Much of the preceding discussion of the workplace, computerisation – and the critical remarks about dehumanised work – has been in terms of the modern factory. But since modern manufacturing now has links with the service sector, scientific research and educational establishments, it seems important to call attention to the trends which Orwell so well portrayed as the processes of 'thought control' and 'double think' – the predominance of academic and scientific expertise over human autonomy and alternative ways of organising life and material production. The production of knowledge is in fact fast becoming a process parallel to material production in the factory system.

It is now seriously suggested that universities should be organised along the lines of a factory model, a development already described elsewhere.[8] In these models, the recruitment of students is referred to as 'material procurement', recruitment as 'resource planning and development', faculty research and study as 'supply procurement', instructional methods planning as 'process planning', examinations and award credits as 'quality control', instructor evaluation as 'resource maintenance' and graduation as 'deliveries'. The professors and lecturers are of course referred to as 'operators'. Other models have provided for the use of a Frankfurter Algorithm employing multi-criterion problem techniques to measure the rate at which university professors are functioning.

Such developments run alongside systematic attempts to 'scientifically' work out the rate at which people are thinking. It is claimed that pupilary dilations indicate mental effort by showing the remarkable relationship between the levels of complexity of mental arithmetic and the magnitude of dilation during the problem solving processes. In the early 1970s observation of dilation of the pupil when looking at pictures could indicate whether the pictures were 'interesting and attention getting' and had established a distinction between 'seeing' and 'looking'. Thus we find both in the design of hardware and software, and the organisational forms which surround its use, a convergence in many instances to the controls which were highlighted in *Nineteen Eighty-Four*.

There are of course powerful economic and political forces which determine that Orwell's warning of dehumanised labour should come true. Although systems planning is only now beginning to encroach on the organisation of modern industry we must recognise that its introduction is considerably advanced by the corporate decision to restructure production both in technical *and* organisational terms. In manufacturing, as in the public sector, we can see the beginning of a permanent shift away from direct employment towards contract service, witness the mounting examples in electrical maintenance, catering, transport, machine servicing and cleaning. But the trend is not confined to services alone, and as the functions of manufacturing are rationalised into sub-units (using systems planning) whole areas can be sub-contracted out. Some previously vertically integrated industries, for example, have broken down into separate companies operating on contract or commission. In a number of industries, major companies are actually forcing their workers either to establish their own business with redundancy payments – or deliberately allowing substantial areas of the work to go to sub-contractors, often former employees in another guise. Technically, such a pattern of industrial restructuring is made more achievable through the complete integration of manufacturing functions into a corporate planning system – both internal and external to the company concerned – with a communications relay between the factory and the company's most important outside suppliers and sub-contractors carried directly on computers.

For us, these economic trends portray *political* characteristics, and we recognise that the implied restructuring of work organisation is fundamentally connected to a kind of technological imperialism. Today it is a dangerous delusion to view computers as 'revolutionising' our lives. Far from generating social change, they have been mainly used to preserve traditional structures, simply allowing them to operate on a much larger scale. The value of *Nineteen Eighty-Four* is that it focuses our attentions on these powerful and dangerous trends in our society. It is to be hoped, however, that our concern can be transformed into positive action, and result in a powerful and socially conscious movement to ensure that technologies and systems are designed to liberate human beings – rather than the other way round.

Chapter 8

Paul Lashmar
Information as Power

*'I do not believe that the kind of society I describe will arrive, but I
believe that something resembling it could arrive.'* Orwell.

We live, we are told, in a stable, democratic society where repression
is something you hear about on the news. It happens elsewhere. As a
result, there is something of a superior tone about the British attitude
to fears of Big Brother. And of course it would be ludicrous to suggest
that we *are* living in a country that bears much resemblance to
Airstrip One, the nightmarish, all-embracing, totalitarian state of
Nineteen Eighty-Four. Nevertheless, Orwell's fantasy was overwhelmingly accurate in identifying technology as the tool that would
be utilised by the State to impose its political will. Indeed Orwell's
only failure was to underestimate just how comprehensive the
technological advance of the next three decades would be. Readers of
the novel's first printing may have chilled at the prospect of
telescreens controlled by Big Brother; yet the security forces have at
their disposal today equipment far more sophisticated and far more
intrusive.

The opportunity for the state to develop and test these new tools
came in the period immediately after Orwell completed his
manuscript. The retreat from Empire may have seemed ignominious,
but the security experts returned with immense experience in the
control of civilian populations and the suppression of dissidents. On
the home front it was a time too for the state to refine a complex
internal security system.

In Britain, extensive government secrecy masks from public view
many of the activities of the 'security services' – from the Special
Branch to MI5, MI6 and the government's Communications
Headquarters in Cheltenham. This contrasts strongly with America,
whose technology and security agencies are similar to our own, but
whose Freedom of Information Act has allowed occasional light to
be shed. Such insights led Senator Frank Church to comment in 1975
on the technology available to the security services that 'at any time it
could be turned on the American people ... the capacity is there to
make tyranny total'.[1]

In Britain, this technology, and the powers to use it, have been acquired for quite lawful reasons, the public in general believing that the security services have a legitimate task to perform. But the chief constables, generals and the anonymous men who run the security services always seek to extend their powers, recent examples including the Prevention of Terrorism Act and the Police and Criminal Evidence Bill. Whether the *application* of these powers is legitimate is another question.

As far back as 1976, in *The Technology of Political Control*,[2] it was suggested that we were moving towards a new state model, a form of 'Strong State' different either from Fascism or a military dictatorship, yet increasingly authoritarian and contemptuous of human rights. The roots of this Strong State are also said to lie in traditional Right wing values of paternalism, authoritarianism and the current government. It is in fact unnerving to consider how far we have moved along the road towards the Strong State in the past seven years. With the current problems of unemployment and recession, and the possibility of serious civil disobedience, perhaps involving riots similar to those of 1981, it is unlikely that the heroine of the Falklands confrontation would flinch from using all the resources of the state to maintain control.

Continuing Wars

In Airstrip One the population has its emotional energy fully directed towards the external enemy, whether Eastasia or Eurasia. Constant and limited wars with these two countries allow restrictions on the population that would not be tolerated otherwise. It is similarly through the justification of various 'wars' that some of the undemocratic practices of the British State go unchallenged – and practices theoretically redundant in a peacetime society are not only maintained but quietly reinforced. Their common target is said to be the 'enemy within', and it is possible to pinpoint three separate 'wars' that the British State has been involved in for many years: an ideological war, the 'war against crime' and the undeclared war in Northern Ireland.

At the time Orwell was writing in the late 1940s, Britain was entering a new phase in the *ideological war* which has been raging since the turn of the century and is still with us today. The 'Cold War' has provided the British security forces with much of its experience and raison d'etre, whether fighting Marxist dissidents in the colonies or unmasking Communist spies within its own ranks. The ideological war with Communism now casts the shadow of nuclear war over us.

It has justified a civil defence programme which doubles as an Emergency Powers Act, putting authority in the hands of a small group of politicians and military leaders at a time of national crisis. The plans for civil defence show that in an emergency, the first to be rounded up would be anybody previously categorised as a 'subversive'. There are believed to be 20,000 names on the arrest lists maintained by M15.[3]

The police vision of a *war against crime* reveals the siege mentality of officers moving steadily away from the communities which they are supposed to serve. A typical report from one London Community Relations Council amplifies this:

'In a recent television programme Commander Adams made a very revealing statement when explaining why he had not told the Police Community Liaison Committee that the Special Patrol Group (SPG) were coming into Lambeth. He said: "No good general ever declares his forces in a prelude to any kind of attack." He thus confirmed what [the community groups] had begun to think – that the ideas underlying Brixton's police methods are more akin to those of an army [against the community] than anything else.'[4]

In the process, the police have managed to achieve something that is quite hard to do – shake the faith of the public in their competence. Public sympathy with the police is a fundamentally English thing, few other countries viewing their police with such benign eyes. But the police have developed a complacency and arrogance that is now working against them; too frequently the attitude of senior police officers indicates that they think only they know best.

Thirdly, the 'troubles', or the *real war* in Northern Ireland, has provided the British state with a well trained anti-insurgency force. It is as though part of the British Isles has been cordoned off and turned into an experiment in population control. The British Army and the Royal Ulster Constabulary have been at the forefront in developing sophisticated political warfare techniques – from the passive to the active to the illegal. Invisible, passive surveillance involves telephone tapping, mail opening, 'tailing' and the compilation of massive intelligence files, with impressive details of half Ulster's population of 1.5 million recorded on the Army's intelligence computer at Lisburn Barracks. The obviously active role has been street and house-to-house searches, arrests, and internment. And with the use of illegal torture on suspects already proven, there are now repeated, 'proud' leaks that the SAS have long been commissioned to assassinate 'known' terrorists.

Some of the British Intelligence activities in Northern Ireland and in Eire have also included covert action previously only used against hostile foreign countries. There is overwhelming evidence that British Intelligence has instigated and been involved in bombings, bank robberies, kidnappings and even murder. One of the most famous incidents was in Dublin in 1976 when two bombs were planted and exploded the day before the Irish parliament was due to vote on tougher measures against Republican terrorists. It was generally believed that the proposals would be voted down; the bombs resulted in the measures being massively approved. The planting of these bombs would have been a stupid act by the IRA, and there subsequently came to light evidence that a British Intelligence officer was involved.[5]

In *Nineteen Eighty-Four*, after his arrest, Winston Smith is subjected to torture to break him down. But that torture was not purely physical, and it was used not as punishment or revenge. Its purpose was to make him accept that his torturers had complete control. Smith's prison environment is classic sensory deprivation: windowless buildings, lights on 24 hours a day, food given erratically. The RUC, trained by British Intelligence officers, operated a not dissimilar system of interrogation at Castlereagh Barracks. Although physical violence was extensively used as in *Nineteen Eighty-Four*, its aim was psychological breakdown.[6] The targets were two-fold: to obtain information and get confessions of involvement in crime. This torture was finally stopped in 1979 after an extensive campaign by Amnesty International but it remains an illuminating example of the methods the British state is prepared to sanction against its own citizens in times of strife.

Since the path of torture was officially closed, the Army and the Royal Ulster Constabulary have taken a course straight out of Lt-Gen. Frank Kitson's *Low Intensity Operations*, a book based on experience gained in dealing with terrorists in former colonies. Over the last three years the RUC have made extensive use of the 'supergrass' system to cripple terrorist groups. Supergrasses were first used by Scotland Yard in the early 1970s to deal with an armed robbery crimewave: an arrested criminal would give evidence against his former colleagues in return for a much shorter sentence, and a new identity.

The initial use of a single supergrass's evidence to obtain a conviction was soon criticised. Generally, it now takes the evidence of two supergrasses and corroborating evidence to make a case on the mainland. But in Northern Ireland the state is prepared to 'put away' alleged terrorists on the basis of *one* supergrass's evidence. These people are also given immunity, a practice long stopped on the mainland. As a result, the law in Northern Ireland is widely considered to be in a state of farce, some political cases still being tried in 'Diplock' courts with no juries at all.

This is pure *1984*. In Ulster the laws are not made for the community for the community's own good, but are drafted at the behest of hard-pressed security services to improve their success rate. In Airstrip One there were no laws, only edicts from above. And it's not just Ulster. The desperate measures to deal with terrorism have spread to the mainland, with the Prevention of Terrorism Act applied to the whole of the United Kingdom. This allows exclusion orders, internal deportation and lengthy detention.

The Technology

In Airstrip One, we can assume that if the surveillance was so extensive as to strike fear into the hearts of its citizens, and result in a high 'disappearance' rate, then it must have been extremely labour-intensive. But the equipment now being developed and available in Britain is designed to minimalise the labour of surveillance. Take the modern equivalent of the ubiquitous 'telescreens'. Two-way home computers with visual display units will be in many homes in the near future, but they will not be used as a sort of advanced two-way mirror. In a British totalitarian state, the information collected on the data banks of grocery companies, credit card companies and banks would be equally revealing without being nearly as labour-intensive as a telescreen.

The telephone, a principal tool of the security services, has no place in Airstrip One because informal communication is implicitly banned. In Britain in 1984, however, the authorities have the ability to monitor all calls, long or short distance, home or abroad, and enormous resources with which to do it. The surprising extent of state telephone tapping was hinted at when London's secret 'Tinkerbell' telephone tapping centre was exposed in 1981.[7] As a result of the public and parliamentary outcry, Lord Diplock was despatched by the government to inquire into the use of telephone tapping by the Post Office for the police and security services. In his report, he proclaimed that 4,210 warrants were issued for the tapping of telephone lines between 1969 and 1979, but he had gone through a random selection of tapping cases and concluded that the public could set their minds at rest.[8] Most of these are in fact likely to be for 'political' surveillance.[9]

In May, 1983, the European Court of Human Rights ruled against the British government's right to telephone tap. In a case brought by James Malone, an antique dealer charged in 1977 with handling stolen goods but subsequently acquitted, it emerged that at least one telephone conversation of his had been tapped. The court ruled that the tapping of telephones was a breach of Articles 8 ('right to respect for private life and correspondents') and 13 ('availability of an effective remedy before a National Authority') of the European Convention of Human Rights. Even so, the ease with which the British state can telephone tap will be much enhanced by the new 'System X' generation of new technology telephone exchanges, making it almost impossible, except for a few 'secure' people, to know whether a telephone is tapped.[10]

Mail as an informal means of communication has no place in Airstrip One. But our police and security services benefit from the Post Office's willingness to operate a mail opening service, an activity run from its Investigation Department in the City of London.[11] For many years, the Communist Party and other Left wing groups have assumed that their mail is inspected, and although the equipment is sophisticated there are still tell-tale signs: sometimes mail arrives clumsily resealed or is accidentally 'returned to sender'. By contrast, surveillance microphones or bugging devices are rare in Britain compared with Airstrip One. Nonetheless, the 'infinity' microphone wired into a home telephone can relay even conversations in the room itself, whilst the thorough surveillance by bugs of the Patriotic Front delegates to the 1980 Lancaster House talks about Zimbabwe is one of the four documented examples.

In London and at some other key locations the Orwellian concept of 'Big Brother is watching you' is most vividly echoed by the video cameras placed in commanding positions. Their use is primarily for traffic control; but they can also be employed to monitor political demonstrations or street activity. At present, 145 cameras cover 200 square miles of London as part of Central Integrated Traffic Control scheme (CITRAC), which is run jointly by the police and the Greater London Council. There is also a secondary network of cameras specifically for crowd control run by the Metropolitan Police alone. Less is known about this system except that it has cameras overlooking Whitehall, Parliament Square, Trafalgar Square, Grosvenor Square and Marble Arch. Some of the cameras are infra red and can 'see' in the dark.[12]

The police also make use of privately owned cameras for surveillance. Security staff at Charing Cross Hospital in Hammersmith, for example, informed me that the police used the security cameras on top of the tall building to observe demonstrations. These cameras are capable of identifying individuals at a distance of a mile. Meanwhile, the Metropolitan Police Jet Ranger helicopter frequently seen and irritatingly heard at many London demonstrations carries a powerful video camera on board – capable of a very precise resolution. Other cameras on main roads around the country act as the 'eyes' for intelligent computers capable of reading and recording car registration numbers.

Computers

Perhaps the greatest difference when comparing the technology of Airstrip One and Britain, 1984, is that Orwell did not foresee the use of the computer. The vast computer system in the hands of the police and security services, and the over 200 data banks used by central government departments, contain the potential, if linked, to provide an extremely detailed analysis of our personal lives. In surveillance terms, they are the telescreens of the real 1984; and the kind of details which could be revealed were hinted at in a recent court case.

In May, 1983, the Inland Revenue obtained a successful prosecution against Richard Jones, managing director of a large container company. Jones claimed he was living in America while in fact he was living here, and the Inland Revenue produced details of his credit card transactions to prove the point. In one case, for instance, where he had claimed to have written a letter in Miami on a particular day, it was shown that he had used his credit card in a DIY shop in Stamford Bridge, West London.[13]

Most concern, however, surrounds the police use of computers, partly because these are deliberately shrouded in mystery. The Police National Computer, at the centre of the network, provides a nationwide 'rapid system' data service to 800 local terminals, and includes such information as the names of known criminals and over 23 million registered vehicle owners. But it is increasingly likely to also contain 'intelligence', in the sense of personal details or allegations about individuals listed. Records of vehicles, for example, can have special information 'flagged' to them all – owing insertion or retrieval only by the Special Branch. One example of this would be a person's membership of a pressure group. Amongst the 'criminal' names there are also those of people simply *charged* with offences, whilst the 'wanted/missing' section can easily be used to watch 'suspects'.[14]

At a local level, police 'collaters', who gather 'soft' information – snippets of gossip and rumour together with observations on the activities of known criminals and the suspicions of local police officers – are also beginning to move their stores of information from card indexes to computers. Even the chairman of the Association of Chief Police Officers' Committee on police computers, Stanley Bailey, admits there are problems about finding the middle ground between factual information and intelligence.[15] But the Home Office remains anxious that as many forces as possible install computers, and the first of a new generation of 'major incident' computers, codenamed MIRIAM, was being installed in Essex Police head-quarters during July, 1983.[16]

Sinister as they may be as political tools, police computers are at the same time notoriously insecure. Every year examples of widespread abuse leak out, and police officers have quite frequently sold or given information from the PNC or DVLC to unauthorised people. In one case an officer sold the addresses of car numbers at 50p a time to the owners of a casino so they could canvas rival customers.[17] It is also widely known that detective agencies and the security departments of companies employ ex-police officers because they can gain access to criminal records through their old colleagues. In October, 1981, *The Observer* showed how highly confidential information on police computer and intelligence files was being disclosed over the phone to anybody who knows one of at least three childishly simple methods.[18]

The Thought Police

The most insidious of police uses of computers, however, is by the Special Branch, whose national files are kept on the Metropolitan Police's 'C' Department crime computer in London. The Special Branch are the nearest thing we have to the 'thought police'. They are concerned with politically related crime, act on behalf of the more anonymous M15 and M16 and spend much of their time in surveillance and the collection of information on individuals. The official definition of their work is that they are concerned with offences against the security of state, with terrorist and subversive organisations, with assisting the uniformed police with the main-tenance of order, with certain protection duties, with keeping watch on airports and seaports, and making enquiries about aliens, but the Special Branch *are* Britain's political police.

There are approximately 1300 Special Branch officers around the country, half of them based in London, although the government is typically secretive about their activities. It took a long campaign by MP Robin Cook to obtain the exact figure for officers, whilst this pressure also forced some Chief Constables to make brief reference in their Annual Reports to the Special Branch officers under their control for the very first time. It is only occasionally, in fact, that any information emerges about the type of intelligence collected in the Special Branch's 1.3 million files.[19] When Chief Constable John

Anderson ordered the Special Branch in Devon and Cornwall to weed its files, their political surveillance included reports on anti-nuclear activists, opponents of blood sports, members of Anti-Apartheid and people who, for example, had been sent to dine with Tony Benn.[20] These are the 'enemies of the state' in 1984. Despite supposedly stringent security measures *The Observer* also obtained details from an individual's Special Branch file.[21] The file was on Hugh Geach, a pillar of respectability in his home town in Kent where he has stood as an SDP Councillor. It seems that Mr Geach, who has no criminal record, attracted the attention of the Special Branch because of his involvement in the Anti-Apartheid 'Stop the Springbok Tour' in 1970. He is still on the computer.

The National Council for Civil Liberties has campaigned hard for the registration of *all* state computers but has failed so far. The Data Protection Bill, published just before Christmas 1982, exempted from registration all national security systems, including those held by Special Branch. Pressure brought to bear on the British government by Data Protection Commissioners from nine other Western European countries has so far been to no avail, as the Bill currently stands there is no reason why your medical records, stored in one computer, cannot be linked to the Special Branch.[22]

Above the Special Branch in the security hierarchy is *M15*, which functions as the internal security service, although it has no statutory legal basis and operates on a directive issued in 1952. The most routine work for M15 officers is the carrying out of 'positive vetting', checking the security clearances of thousands of people working in government or in companies which carry our secret government contracts. Their work also involves closely watching the activities of foreign diplomats who might be spying and potential terrorists. But M15, together with Special Branch, also keeps surveillance on hundreds of thousands of people whose greatest sin is nothing more than being politically active, particularly in groups on the left of the political spectrum.

M15's files are kept on a massive and powerful computer code-named MOD-X and kept in Mount Row, Mayfair.[23] It is the biggest government computer in Britain, twice the size of the PNC and it also has the Orwellian capacity to register the names of 20,000 people to be arrested in a time of national emergency.

Finally, it is worth mentioning the involvement of *Government Communications Headquarters* (GCHQ), which also has the ability to listen in to telephone calls and telex messages going in and out of this country. Suspicion that GCHQ have been listening to internal calls has been underlined by revelations that DSD, GCHQ's Australian protégé, has been evading restrictions on the tapping of phones by other agencies. The *National Times* obtained secret Australian Government papers that showed that DSD was tapping the phone calls of political figures, including Australian MPs.[24] The computers being developed by GCHQ are believed to be able to understand a limited spoken human vocabulary, in particular responding to key words.

To what extent, then, are the state organisations of political surveillance pushing us further towards George Orwell's worst fears? Civil libertarians have achieved some successes, for instance, over the dropping of the Protection of Information Bill after the public outcry over the Anthony Blunt affair. But the losses have been mounting. Not only has little progress been made towards removing existing, outdated laws like the pervasive Official Secrets Act, but further legislation like the Data Protection Bill, which endangers our privacy still further, is about to enter the statute book.

The forces of law and order feign amazement at suggestions of abuse of their existing power, whilst pushing for their strengthening. Increasingly as the economic crisis and unemployment deepens, their methods are becoming harsher and more repressive. A similar situation exists with the security services. As a Labour Party discussion puts it:

'We do not say that such services should be abolished. There are genuine threats and actual acts of espionage and terrorism which security agencies of various sorts must combat in the interests of individual and collective liberty. However the obvious danger is that the security services may drift into practices that undermine and endanger the very freedoms they are supposed to defend.'[25]

It is fundamental to maintaining a democratic society that decisions should be made by a well-informed population. This is made particularly hard by the secretive nature of the British State. Why then is British government so secretive? Is it because they realise that information is the new wealth and that wealth is power? Could it be that they realise that if they were both well informed and their illusions about the British state demystified, the people might want to take a more active part in running their own lives?

BILL EVANS

Chapter 9

Colin Ward
Big Brother Drives a Bulldozer

Orwell's book was not, as some people said at the time, the nightmare of a dying man. It was a long-premeditated polemical satire which brought together a whole range of the themes that had preoccupied its author for many years. The critic Matthew Hodgart recommended a re-reading of *Nineteen Eighty-Four* every ten years or so for what he called the pure delight of seeing real life parody Orwell's fantasy or support his insights. This is certainly true of the larger themes of the book, and equally so of the apparently minor ones.

Four of these, intimately linked together in Orwell's mind, were: nostalgia, environmental decay, the *trahison des clercs* – in the sense of the betrayal of ordinary human aspirations by the educated classes – and the superiority of the values by which poor people scrape by in life – through self-help and mutual aid. If there is hope, it lies with the proles.

Nostalgia is one of the great contemporary diseases. It isn't, as the joke says, what it used to be. It was certainly never to universal, particularly at the time when *Nineteen Eighty-Four* was written. Orwell's friends used to regard it as a harmless eccentricity that he collected curious bits of junk and drank his Typhoo tea from a Victorian commemorative mug. Today, the survivors among them all, no doubt, have collections of old mugs on their stripped pine peasant dressers and think them too precious to drink from. Winston Smith, like his creator, yearning for a lost past, is hungry for the physical evidence of the history that has been abolished. He cherishes the bound album of cream-laid paper that he bought from a frowsy junk shop in a slummy quarter of town, the place where he later gets scraps of 'beautiful rubbish' like the glass paperweight and the steel engraving of St Clement's Dane.

'The world of today', explains Goldstein in the samizdat book within the novel, 'is a bare, hungry, dilapidated place compared with the world that existed before 1914,' (slightly shaky social history of course), 'and still more so if compared with the imaginary future to which the people of that period looked forward. In the early twentieth century, the vision of a future society unbelievably rich, leisured, orderly and efficient in a glittering antiseptic world of glass and steel and snow-white concrete – was part of the consciousness of nearly every literate person.'

Nearly every literate person, faced by the real 1984, hates the cracked glass, rusty steel and stained concrete world and is in the grip of Winston's nostalgia for the world we have lost. Every second rate building, from the Victorian work-house to the 1930s factory on the by-pass, has been 'listed' as characteristic of its period (though this never precludes its demolition on a public holiday when there is no one in the office to receive a complaint). The junk shop is now called 'Things of Yesteryear' or 'Granny's Treasure Box', and the bits of beautiful rubbish have become bygones, if not antiques; even the enamelled advertisements, Bovril jars and ginger beer bottles loved by Orwell are now treasured.

Winston Smith has a recurring dream of the Golden Country; we turned *The Country Diary of an Edwardian Lady* and *Life in the English Country House* into best-selling books. Even our Prime Minister, a product of the managerial and technocratic rather than the patrician generation, advocates what she regards as Victorian values. What does it mean, this universal nostalgia for a make believe past? The spread of nostalgia from a foible in 1948 to an obsession in 1984 has several explanations. The most obvious is that we have slowly moved from living in the present to disliking it, and from happily anticipating the future to dreading it.

The environmental background of Orwell's book, with its monolithic Ministry buildings, Victory Mansions and the prole districts beyond, was always explained by friends like Julian Symons as a mirror of the shabby, peeling, post-war London of 1948, with its bomb sites and makeshift repairs. Winston Smith wanders 'in the vague brown-coloured slums to the north and east of what had once been St Pancras station ... up a cobbled street of little two-storey houses with battered doorways which gave straight onto the pavement ... perhaps a quarter of the windows in the street were broken and boarded up.' Barraged with statistics on the telescreen proving that the people of *1984* had more food, more clothes and better houses than those of 50 years ago, Winston looks at the reality of 'decaying, dingy cities where underfed people shuffled to and fro in leaky shoes, in patched-up nineteenth-century houses that smelt always of cabbage and bad lavatories.'

Orwell's description of the prole sector of the city isn't just 1948. For any of us can recognise in it the decaying inner city districts of a dozen British cities in the real 1984, even in the particular bit of London that Winston wanders into. Every city has such pockets of environmental neglect, left to rot until wholesale demolition and rebuilding becomes inevitable. The demographic and industrial centre of gravity has moved elsewhere; the residents of these areas are superfluous to the economy.

But between 1948 and 1984, an enormous official bulldozer of redevelopment did begin to eliminate one such district after another, replacing those Victorian terrace houses with the local authority's Victory Mansions. The fact that so many remain is simply because the money ran out. As a group of urban historians recently put it: 'In building a new world through urban renewal the planners broke the continuity between past and present and left the "redeveloped" citizen without familiar urban roots. An urban utopia it certainly did not become as damp, boredom, vandalism and garbage undermined the urban vision: having demolished slums which stood for a century, we constructed homes which lasted a decade."

Generations of inner city children have grown up in the atmosphere of dereliction and decay that Orwell described, in the enormous time lag between the death sentence on the area and the decanting of its population to a place where they would rather not be. One well documented city in this respect is Sunderland, where Norman Dennis has described the devastating effect of policy in his books *People and Planning* and *Public Participation and Planners' Blight*. He has shown (and his examples could be replicated in any other British city) how, in the making of decisions affecting their environment, the perceptions of ordinary poor inhabitants (we can equate them with Orwell's proles) have been left, as a matter of policy, out of the calculation. He talks, in precisely the same tone as Orwell, about Millfield, a district of Sunderland, and the two possible ways of looking at the place. Within the planners' frame of reference, he says, the place is 'a collection of shabby, mean and dreary house, derelict back lanes, shoddy-fronted shops and broken pavements, the whole unsightly mess mercifully ill-lit.' But he asks us to look at it from a second point of view, which Orwell would have grasped immediately but which was invisible to the council and its professional employees. From the point of view of a 60-year-old woman living there, he says:

'Millfield is Bob Smith's which she thinks (probably correctly) is the best butcher's in the town; George McKeith's wet-fish shop and Peary's fried-fish shop about which she says the same with equal justification; Maw's hot pies and peas, prepared on the premises; the Willow Pond public house, in which her favourite nephew organises the darts and dominoes team; the Salvation Army band in a nearby street every Sunday and waking her with carols on Christmas morning; her special claim to attention at the grocer's because her niece worked there for several years; the spacious cottage in which she was born and brought up, which she now owns, has improved, and which has not in her memory had defects which have caused either her or her neighbours discernible inconvenience (but which has some damp patches which make it classifiable as a "slum dwelling"); the short road to the cemetery where she cares for the graves of her mother, father and brother; her sister's cottage across the road – she knows that every week-day at 12.30 a hot dinner will be ready for her when she comes home from work; the bus route which will take her to the town centre in a few minutes; the homes of neighbours who since her childhood have helped her and whom she has helped, church, club and workplace within five minutes' walk; and, in general (as is said) "every acre sweetened by the memory of the men who made us".'[2]

The supreme irony of Norman Dennis' attempt to put the point of view of ordinary citizens into the politics of the environment, is as A. H. Halsey remarks, 'that when a person like Norman Dennis protests against the emerging tyranny of government with the authentic voice of a deeply-rooted English socialism, he is heard with approval by Sir Keith Joseph and dismissed as a nuisance by the Labour establishment.'

In terms of Orwell's book it illustrates the chasm, in environmental perception, between the Party and the proles. And it is a story that can be repeated from every city. I met, for example, Mr Simms, who lived in the last house in Albert Street, Canton, Cardiff, to have curtains at its windows. He had been born in that street and his grandparents had lived there. He belonged to that not inconsiderable group of poor owner-occupiers who, in the 1940s and 1950s, had managed to buy, as sitting tenants, the houses they had rented for generations. His was not an unfit house. Piecemeal improvements over the years had given it a bathroom, water closet, hot water supply and so on. But it, and the street, and the surrounding streets, were being emptied and demolished in a rolling programme devised by Cardiff Corporation. The council was, in fact, selling the land to a private developer who was building new houses for sale at prices which were many times the compensation that the council was going to pay him. His former neighbour had been paid £1,800. If this sum was simply regarded as a mortgage deposit on one of the new houses, whose floor area and whose gardens were considerably smaller, he would never have been accepted as a mortgagee because his income was low and his age was 53.

The council was offering him a tenancy in one of the new estates on the fringe of the city, but this he told me, was of no use to him. He loathed the status of tenant, he thought the rents were too high, he ridiculed the design and he despised what he regarded as the humiliation of having to apply for a rent rebate and supplementary benefit when he became 65, because he saw this as seeking charity from some officious bureaucrat. Life, he thought, would be hideously expensive on the new estate, and he compared prices at the new high-rent supermarket there with those at the low-rent corner shop in Canton. And what, he asked, was going to happen to the woman who kept the corner shop? She had been deprived of her livelihood. But so had Mr Simms himself, for his job involved him in getting up at four and walking down to work to open the dock gates for the lorries. Quite apart from the fares, there was no means of transport from the new estate at that hour.

So the council, in one operation, was taking away his friends and neighbours, his home, and his job, was putting up his family's cost of living, taking away his garden, his hobby, and even the security he thought he had procured for himself and his wife in their old age. And it was doing this so as to make a profit from selling the land to a speculative builder who also expected to make a profit. 'I don't know,' Mr Simms said to me quietly, 'how the Corporation can be so cruel.' In his view the council had waged a war of attrition against a whole community, slowly and deliberately running down a whole neighbourhood and its amenities. No wonder the architect Bruce Allsop remarks that 'it is astonishing with what savagery planners and architects are trying to obliterate working-class cultural and social patterns. Is it because many of them are first generation middle-class technosnobs?'[3]

This is a shrewd question, and it leads to a further reflection on the incidental parallels between Orwell's satire and life. The new governing class in *Nineteen Eighty-Four*, the Party members who man the Ministry of Truth, the Ministry of Love, the Ministry of Peace and the Ministry of Plenty, are drawn from 'bureaucrats, scientists, technicians, trade-union organisers, publicity experts, sociologists, teachers, journalists and professional politicians. These people, whose origins lay in the salaried middle class and the upper grades of the working class, had been shaped and brought together by the barren world of monopoly industry and centralised government.' Compared with earlier ruling elites they are hungrier, not for luxury, but for pure power, and are more ruthless in crushing opposition.

Is it far-fetched to equate Orwell's men of power with the shapers of the urban environment in our real 1984? Consider the experience of Newcastle-upon-Tyne. The celebrated Labour leader of its council was T. Dan Smith, who determined to make that city 'the New Brasilia'. In his memoirs he describes how 'I hired a Rapide aircraft to make flying visits to see candidates for our new appointment of a

Planning Officer ... Local government had moved from a parish pump era into the big business league ...'.[4] The Planning Officer he found was Wilfred Burns, a 'forceful' character, who declared that 'the dwellers in a slum area are almost a separate race of people, with different values, aspirations and ways of living ... Most people who live in slums have no views on their environment at all.'[5] Furthermore, 'when we are dealing with people who have no initiative or civic pride, the task, surely, is to break up such groupings even though the people seem to be satisfied with their miserable environment and seem to enjoy an extrovert social life in their own locality.'[6]

The historian of the post-war redevelopment of British cities, Alison Ravetz, notes that 'a major feature of the New Brasilia that Burns created, to the satisfaction both of Smith and his Conservative successors, was a motorway ring, part of the national trunk road system, which formed a wall inside which were impressive precincts for council offices, commerce and education. Those who were about to lose their homes or livelihoods to make way for the new polytechnic were issued with a free booklet explaining the importance of higher education for the future prosperity and leisure of the town.'[7] Burns, of course, went on to become Sir Wilfred, and the central government's chief planner.

The 'extrovert social life' that he discerned in the 'miserable environment' of the prole sector of the city has been killed off by the new hard men of the reconstructed city; and although fortunes were made by speculators in the sinister alliance between the planning industry and property developers, the outstanding feature of the urban landscape of 1984 is that the cities have been rebuilt in the interests of the managerial class, both public and private. Orwell was convinced that the new technocratic elite (analysed in a book he disliked, but which greatly influenced him, James Burnham's *The Managerial Revolution*) were not interested in capital accumulation, nor necessarily in capitalism at all, but in the exercise of power, and the rebuilt city reflects this. It represents the shift from a fine-grained to a coarse-grained environment.

This is obvious in the surface texture: the change from small-scale buildings with a lot of visual interest and variety to large-scale megaliths – Orwell's world of glass and steel and snow-white concrete in its shabby reality – with much less to occupy the eye. The coarse, crude slab-like character of post-war building slaps you in the face in every British city, from pavement to skyline. It is also apparent in the economic and social pattern of the city. All those small-scale trades and services which provided the enormous variety of marginal specialised occupations which were one of the reasons why people congregated in cities in the first place, disappear because the high rents of new buildings could not be sustained by the turnover of small businesses depending on low overheads. This process has been documented in London, in Birmingham, and most recently in Glasgow, where a recent study of the decline of work opportunities comments that: 'perhaps more serious in its consequences was the death of the hundreds of small enterprises whose low levels of capital and low overheads, in brick backyard or railway viaduct premises destroyed by demolition, denied them the possibility of relocation.'[8]

It obviously affects homelessness too. The gradual disappearance of cheap rented accommodation, boarding houses and common lodging houses, has meant that there is nowhere for the poor and homeless. Hence the growing 'problem' of homeless single people in the cities. There are more people sleeping rough in London today than in, for instance, New York, where there are still cheap run-down properties, and consequently *somewhere* for people to sleep at all levels of wealth and poverty.

The epitaph on the replanned cities of 1984 was written a decade earlier by Jon Gower Davies. 'Planning in our society,' he wrote, 'is in essence the attempt to inject a radical technology into a conservative and highly inegalitarian economy. The impact of planning on this society is rather like that of the education system on the same society; it is least onerous and most advantageous to those who are already well off or powerful, and it is most onerous and least advantageous to those who are relatively powerless or relatively poor. Planning is, in its effect on the socio-economic structure, a highly regressive form of indirect taxation.'[9] Small wonder that the poor, too are enveloped in nostalgia. They are grieving for a lost home. For the managers, this is irrelevant. Nowadays nobody starves, do they?

The heart of Orwell's book is not the reshaping of Winston's mind so that, with befuddled tears of joy he finds that he, too, loves Big Brother. It is his earlier discovery of the difference between the Party members and the proles. It suddenly occurs to him that the proles were not loyal to a party or a country or an idea, but 'they were loyal to one another. For the first time in his life he did not despise the proles or think of them merely as an inert force which would one day spring to life and regenerate the world. *The proles had stayed human.*' (My italics). It wasn't worth attempting to indoctrinate the proles with the Party ideology; they weren't spied on through telescreens, the Thought Police didn't bother with them, and even the civil police interfered with them very little. The Party's sexual puritanism did not apply to them, and among them was 'a whole world-within-a-world of thieves, bandits, prostitutes, drug-peddlers and racketeers of every description.' It was to their 'black market' and 'free market' that you went for things in chronic short supply, like shoe laces or razor blades. The proles, in fact, were a kind of urban peasantry, and 'left to themselves, like cattle let lose upon the plains of Argentina, they had reverted to a style of life that appeared to be natural to them, a sort of ancestral pattern.'

This is a curious pre-echo of current preoccupations with the significance of the 'black economy' and the 'informal economy', which have arisen partly because we are faced in 1984 with the prospect of permanent large-scale unemployment, and partly because those in secure employment are encouraged to believe that they are supporting a vast army of scroungers. The most interesting projections into the future of current trends are those in a well-known paper by Ray Pahl and Jay Gershuny,[10] who see as one possibility (it is already with us) the creation of a dual labour market. On the one hand is a high technology sector with high wages, and on the other a low wage, fluctuating and unstable sector where the workers 'will expect to augment their wages through tips and fiddles'. They see this as providing the ingredients for 'a nasty, increasingly inegalitarian world', and below this dual labour market 'the informal economy will flourish uncontrolled, and perhaps uncontrollable. This would be a world of *mafiosi*, of big bosses and little crooks.'

As an alternative, or consequence of this, they see a situation in which 'the state, fearful of the unstable situation in the first scenario, increases its power of surveillance and control. It attempts to enforce taxation and employment legislation by increasing the penalties for non-compliance, and by bolstering the police force and other law-enforcing agencies. It keeps up employment in the formal sector by spending the increased tax yield on more public services, and developing a larger bureaucracy ... People would feel much like those caught in the "socialism" of Poland or Czechoslovakia.' There are plenty of Orwellian parallels here, and the authors see both forecasts as extremely disagreeable and unpleasant.

But Pahl's more recent researches throw a different light on the way some poor people do make do and get by in the margins or interstices of the economy of 1984.[11] His case histories belong, not to the inner city, but to the urban fringe, in a place which, he says, simply appears to the middle-class visitor as 'an ugly and polluted industrial wasteland.' He examines what Orwell calls a reversion to an ancestral pattern and what he calls 'a curious anomaly of a section of the working class which has not been fully socialised into industrial capitalism and which still has something of the preindustrial English individualism in its culture.' Pahl's Mr and Mrs Parsons, like Orwell's unreformed proles, 'live in a familiar world of friends and relations ... Neighbours too, link into a tightly knit social world.' Mr Parsons has a low paid morning job in the formal economy, but Mr Simpson is unemployed. 'Aged 33 he is unlikely to get a job again.' His wife works informally at home in the hidden economy, assembling electrical components. The children help her. 'It's slave labour,' she says. But her husband goes off with rod, gun and ferret. 'Yes, he goes poaching. We get everything illegally,' Mrs Simpson laconically remarks.

Like Winston Smith, looking yearningly at the solidarity of the proles, Pahl observes that 'there is a well-established underground culture in the community, supported by the underground economy and focussed on the pubs.' He concludes that 'released from the realm of necessity by capitalism's inevitable desire to continue accumulation and to maintain rates of profit, and protected in the realm of freedom by the need of the state to maintain social control, it seems as if some workers are slipping out of their chains and walking out of the system's front door.' It's another way of phrasing Winston Smith's conclusion that if there *is* hope, it lies with the proles.

Chapter 10

Philip Corrigan
Hard Machines, Soft Messages

George Orwell's 46 years (1903–1950)[1] overlap with mine (from 1942 onwards) only slightly; but these years we both lived through share a highly significant quality – the latter part of the Second World War and the post-war Labour Government. I am convinced[2] that a major impulse towards, and many of the images within, *Nineteen Eighty-Four* flow from this, from what was a lived experience for Orwell, though for me largely body-memory and hardly conscious 'traces'. I do recall as my first sharp memories queueing for coal (mainly dust), the shortages and ration books, and yes, rats. Like Orwell's Winston Smith, I fear rats: the ways they move and how they stare. But what I propose to do here is briefly examine what Orwell tells us of 'everyday life' in *Nineteen Eighty-Four*, and then to look at some features of 'ordinary living' in calender 1984.

Eighty-five per cent of the population of Oceania were 'proles', the rest made up the Inner and Outer Party Members, although we actually know very little about what Orwell called 'those swarming disregarded masses'. 'The great majority of proles did not even have telescreens in their homes', Orwell wrote, and they were not supposed to drink the ubiquitous Party intoxicant Victory Gin, though it seems they could obtain it on the black market. They suffered from shortages, which was also true of the Party shops, and there are a number of general passages which describe life for all (Party and proles):

'It struck him that the truly characteristic thing about modern life was not its cruelty and insecurity, but simply its bareness, its dinginess, its listlessness. Life, if you looked about you, bore no resemblance not only to the lies that streamed out of the telescreens, but even to the ideals that the Party was trying to achieve. Great areas of it, even for a Party member, were neutral and non-political, a matter of slogging through dreary jobs, fighting for a place on the Tube, darning a worn-out sock, cadging a saccharine tablet, saving a cigarette end ... The reality was decaying, dingy cities where underfed people shuffled to and fro in leaky shoes, in patched-up nineteenth century houses that smelt always of cabbage and bad lavatories.' *(pp. 62–3)*

'In any time that he could accurately remember, there had never been quite enough to eat, one had never had socks or underclothes that were not full of holes, furniture had always been battered and rickety, rooms underheated, tube trains crowded, houses falling to pieces, break dark-coloured, tea a rarity, coffee filthy-tasting, cigarettes insufficient – nothing cheap and plentiful except synthetic gin.'

(p.51)

Winston Smith finds the houses of the proles like 'ratholes', their street life 'sordid' and expresses a general distaste and hostility, especially towards the pubs with their 'smell of urine, sawdust, and sour beer'. Like Orwell himself he in fact has a curiously divided view of the proles (i.e., ordinary people). Where they were granted minds, it is claimed that the proles filled them with 'films, football, beer, and above all, gambling', but we are also told that they started work at 12 years old. The dominant metaphor (enshrined by the Party) is that the proles are 'animals'. Yet they are also the source of hope:

'The proles had stayed human. They had not become hardened inside. They had held on to the primitive emotions which he himself had to re-learn by conscious effort.' *(p. 135)*

'... you could share in that future if you kept alive the mind as they kept alive the body ...'*(p.176)*

'The aim of the Party is not merely to prevent men and women from forming loyalties which it might not be able to control. Its real, undeclared purpose was to remove all pleasure from the sexual act. Not love so much as eroticism was the enemy, inside marriage as well as outside it. All marriages between Party members had to be approved by a committee appointed for the purpose, and – though the principle was never clearly stated – permission was always refused if the couple concerned gave the impression of being physically attracted to one another. The only recognized purpose of marriage was to beget children for the service of the Party. Sexual intercourse was to be looked on as a slightly disgusting minor operation, like having an enema.' *(p.56)*

It is implied that the children (within the Party only) were to be conceived by 'artificial insemination (*artsem*, it was called in Newspeak).[1] The proles, as we have seen, 'bred' amongst themselves, whilst the 'poorer quarters swarmed with women who were ready to sell themselves ...' Tacitly the Party was even inclined to encourage prostitution, as an outlet for instincts which could not be altogether suppressed.' Julia later clarifies the situation regarding Party members:

'Unlike Winston, she had grasped the inner meaning of the Party's sexual puritanism. It was not merely that the sex instinct created a world of its own which was outside the Party's control and which therefore had to be destroyed if possible. What was more important was that sexual privation induced hysteria, which was desirable because it could be transformed into war-fever and leader-worship.' *(p.109)*

But Winston had already explained another feature of life for Party members when he missed an evening at the Community Centre for the second time in three weeks.

'In principle a Party member had no spare time, and was never alone except in bed. It was assumed that when he was not working, eating, or sleeping he would be taking part in some kind of communal recreation: to do anything that suggested a taste for solitude, even to go for a walk by yourself, was always slightly dangerous. There was a word for it in Newspeak: *ownlife*, it was called, meaning individualism and eccentricity.' *(p.69)*

Another communal occasion was the canteen at Winston's workplace, which provides a description of the standard cuisine – in contrast with the items (including real coffee) which Julia obtains (from the Inner Party), or with the wine served them by O'Brien. The latter are the only occasions when we are given any sense of major differences between social groups.

And, with respect to living, this is about all that *Nineteen Eighty-Four* has to show us. For the Party members there is a striking similarity in the privations regarding food and drink, and those regarding sexuality; for the proles we have a sense of animalism *and* a kind of mindless nobility of folkishness, with cabbages as a dietary staple, along with beer. Two other features which Orwell highlights are: the change to the metric system (an old man asks for a pint mug in a pub which only serves litres and half litres), and the change to 24 hours time measurement, as announced in the famous opening sentence: 'It was a bright cold day in April, and the clocks were striking thirteen.'[3]

But my main point is that there is so much that *1984* neither says nor shows: it is a curious mixture of the ambiance of War-time London and a particular understanding of 'total' control, for Party members, and 'swarming' ignorance for the proles. Drabness, shortages, privations, drudgery and ugliness are the strongest themes.

Commodities, Pleasures, Having Fun

The strongest silence in Orwell's book (one which makes it a badly distorted mirror image of calendar 1984) concerns consumerism, the fact that pleasures have flourished and been extended since the mid-1950s. Nothing said here ignores the real history of those years (with the periodic rediscoveries of poverty), nor am I denying the present facts regarding unemployment and dependence for millions of the population upon forms of state benefits and support. Equally the ways in which British society is marked by a centralization of power and control should be stressed, along with a particular set of divisions by generations.[4] But all that said, and it needs to be repeatedly stated that Britain is a society constructed around *inequalities*,[5] it is also true to recognise just how limited was Orwell's projection of life – ordinary life – from the War and post-war context in which he wrote.

First, to take the main leisure activity (and one which structures much else of our lives) of television. Developments there have been entirely different from anything discussed or projected by Orwell, who could draw upon television from 1936 to 1939 and the resumption of BBC services in 1946. There are now four available channels which provide tens of thousands with broadcast television; some serials regularly gain audiences of around 18 million people.

I would suggest that television draws to our attention one major change which I do not think has been either sufficiently understood or discussed; that is **scheduling**. I have a strong sense that the last decade or so has begun to see a change which corresponds in significance to the change from task-time to clock-time which historians have identified with the closing decades of the eighteenth and opening quarter of the nineteenth centuries. I sense we are now moving from clock-time to *schedule*-time, and take as one index of this the disappearance of the public clock. I do not ignore the ways in which this could be related to the general ownership of personal watches, but mean by schedule-time (and scheduling generally) the ways in which our days, weeks and years are patterned in terms of kinds of events and occasions.

We are beginning to understand how television scheduling – both horizontally in terms of competition, and vertically in terms of providing a 'flow' for that channel – is related to known patterns within the general audience. Since television schedules us not only in terms of what we watch, but also the consequences of what we watch (what we discuss, debate or know about) and even what we arrange to do to 'fit in' with television, we can see a series of intersecting schedules meshing areas of our life together. I think this could be extended to the relation between work-patterns (within and outside the home) and other social activities involving consumption and leisure.

This scheduling should not be taken to imply that kind of 'massification' which was standard in professional and popular sociology in the 1950s, and which has not quite disappeared in the 1980s. What is important is the recognisable scheduling of different social groups in particular kinds of ways. Although the creation of large supermarkets, for example, and extensive shopping centres or complexes, has diminished other available forms of shop, it has not erased them. No more has the generalisation of certain standard forms of providing food (tinning, freezing, and behind that larger units of production of standard products) diminished a matching series of differently provided kinds of food. It is, on the contrary, the complexity and diversity of scheduling and markets which has to be taken seriously.

For one large group of the population a central experience of 1984 will be that of **waiting** – waiting and queuing – being shifted around different offices, or between professionals. This waiting and queuing is far more generalised than is normally discussed, and many of the changes in the last 20 years (from supermarkets through to one-person buses) have transferred a lot of activity from provider to consumer. Along with a major decline in social provision, which has accelerated greatly in the last ten years, there is now massive experience of privation in the midst of visible affluence. Recent reports have shown the return of a number of diseases related to dietary deficiency, which current government proposals will make much worse.[6] But, as discussions of the difference in the social meaning of unemployment now compared with the 1930s have made very clear, this privation is not either the mass drudgery described by Orwell nor shared and known throughout the country.

The complexity of the advanced (if declining) capitalism within which we live centres upon one feature which Orwell curiously ignores. Over the 30 years since he wrote it it is not exhortation and propaganda which bombards us wherever we are; it is the words and images of publicity, marketing, promotion and advertising. What these soft messages within the hard machine convey is not a simple injunction to buy, but a set of 'ways of living' – a set of expectations and encouragements for consumption and pleasures which have become part of our identities, part of a kind of consumer citizenship. Central to this particular message system is an intensive visualisation of *various sorts* of Good Life which resonates not in this or that advertisement but pervades the image-system, and works also through a wider range of cultural products.

Far from there being sexual privation, the message system of consumption turns upon erotic as much as aesthetic effects. Sexuality is not the game that cannot speak its name, it is everywhere a system of sending messages, a repertoire of promises and possibilities. In fact the regulation is not by producing hysteria, as Julia suggests, the regulation is that most difficult form to comprehend: abundance. And the resulting personal politics tends toward neurosis. To feel 'out of' such a system of plenitude in which consumption does not simply name certain pleasures, but claims that they will guarantee enduring effects, is to feel denied in very important ways.

But such an overview needs immediately to be qualified. For what is remarkable about Orwell's discussion of sexuality is (again) its limits and silences. Sexuality is now much more understood, generally, and a range of practices which he simply took as unproblematically 'normal' have been shown to be one of a variety of possible forms of sexual identity and practice. With all the limits and taboos (clutched together in that curious term 'permissiveness') it is now a more sexually open society than was the case in Orwell's 1948: changes in the forms and availability of contraception (including contraceptive advice) have given far greater control to women over their own bodies. Various forms of different sexuality have also been struggled for as legitimate practices and identities, especially gay men and lesbian women, and along with heterosexuals these have successfully turned back the limiting and constraining notions of masculinity and femininity.

Along with this have come major changes in forms of household, marriage rates, patterns of divorce and re-marriage, co-habitation and collective forms of living which are not addressed at all in *1984*. The novel suggests as normal for Party members either forms of marriage or single residence (whilst proles seem to marry once and stay married) with, as I indicated, the 'subversion' of Julia and Winston's challenge being its promiscuity.

Abundance and Poverty

I want to conclude by trying to gather up the themes which I think accurately describe some dominant features of living reality in calendar 1984 *and* simultaneously point to those features which were not part of Orwell's predictions. One simple emphasis concerns *complexity*, by which I mean the variety of differing markets that schedule people's lives with both consuming goods and good consumption, through the society of the spectacle. Far from television and related visual forms being means of surveillance and observation, they have become the dominant means through which we see ourselves 'placed' in situations of The Good Life.[7] What modern Western societies appear to offer therefore is **abundance**. The Good Life is scheduled around wishing for, enjoying acquiring and using certain goods and participating in certain marketable pleasures, noticeably those of the spectacle.[8] But 'most people' are excluded from the system of plenitude and satisfaction by virtue of not possessing the means to acquire the goods or experience the spectacles. As a result, those with 'the means' (namely money or access to credit) join the queues to plenty (or short circuit such queues with the telephone and the credit card); those without shuffle forward in the bureaucratic mazes, waiting their time, in the wings, so to speak, of the spectacles they can see on the stage.

But the contrast of 'abundance' and 'poverty' does much more than this. First, it declares those who do not 'gain access' to abundance to be failures, socially inept, victims of their own weaknesses and disabilities. Hence the documented differences between mass unemployment now and in the 1930s. It thus drives them into the shadows in terms of social visibility and personal identity. Secondly, and here is the most powerful feature on a global scale, it *automatically* justifies the world as it is. Certain countries (those of the OECD) are 'full of abundance', the rest of the world is 'full of poverty' – both capitalist and socialist countries. What after all are the repeated images used to define the USSR: shortages, queues, a limited range of consumer goods.

By personalizing failures within advanced capitalist countries (and by comparing stereotypes of whole countries and social systems) the image-system breaks fundamentally the social causes of poverty *and* the links between a restricted abundance and the growing misery and restriction for the majority of the world's population. This is a far more effective system of regulation, through apparent consent and agreement, than the coercive forms suggested by Orwell. Bleakness in the real 1984 is therefore not so much about a shortage of goods, as a shortage of ideals and ideas which will break the strangle-hold of the language of abundance and poverty and point to a basis for different ways of living reality.

Chapter 11

Patrick Wright
The Conscription of History

'Who controls the past controls the future: who controls the present controls the past.' Such is the motto of the Party in *Nineteen Eighty-Four*; and it should speak to us directly enough in the really existing 1980s. For time has only confirmed Orwell's suggestion that the past is subject to political manipulation, and not simply in its miserable application to the Soviet bloc.[1] In Britain, the 1980s have already seen enough public invocation of a revamped Imperial past to leave no doubt that here too history is capable of serving interests quite other than those of natural curiosity or scholastic research. Orwell, however, did not rest with the general observation that the past can be reworked and pressed into the service of present political purposes. His novel goes considerably further, identifying three distinct ways in which a sense of the past is maintained within the present, and exploring some possible relations between them. So I shall first describe these before moving on to discuss how formative such public consciousness of history has become to the politics of contemporary Britain.

On one side then, *Nineteen Eighty-Four* gives us history in the **archival** sense – the records on which any analytical understanding of past and present must depend. These are, of course, directly controlled, and we see Winston Smith working at the heart of the process, rewriting old editions of *The Times* around the shifting imperatives of the present and casting previous versions into 'memory holes' which whisk them off to be obliterated in vast, all-devouring furnaces. The archive is relatively easy to control and the Party has indeed taken it over, dissolving and reconstructing it to produce a mirror of its own intentions in the present. This, to take a phrase from the doctoring of old photographs, is airbrush history in the Soviet style. As Orwell's book asks: 'How could you establish even the most obvious fact when there existed no record outside your own memory?[2]

Memory forms a second co-ordinate of Orwell's presentation, and here the picture is significantly different. *Nineteen Eighty-Four* does not suggest that memory has simply been expunged by various techniques of thought control. Instead it is brutally *dislocated* as its social and cultural basis is destroyed. There is terror between people (which makes for silence), and as if this sort of coercion isn't enough the language itself has been systematically impoverished and the environment refashioned in a style which is free of precedent and therefore supports no meanings or associations which are not immediately synchronous with the totalitarian present. As for the public sphere of discussion and communication, it has been made inescapable (the omnipresent and watchful telescreen) and at the same time occupied by an incessant presentation of the monolithic Party line.

In this situation memory is repositioned rather than simply destroyed: it is detached from this regulated everyday life and cast into a limbo in which it can only degenerate further. Winston Smith, to quote an obvious example, can scarcely understand what he remembers of his parents (who disappeared in the earliest purges) because tragedy – being dependent on the care and intimacy of a private sphere which no longer exists – is simply not conceivable as an experience. So memory doesn't just fade away. It becomes a mutilated anomaly, 'a series of bright-lit tableaux – occurring against no background and mostly unintelligible.'

A third element in Orwell's meditation on the political conscription of the past is made up of **objects** and fleeting presences. Here one finds the cherished bits and pieces from the junk shop in the prole quarter – like the notebook which Winston uses as a journal, or the paperweight which is so resonant for him but eventually destroyed by the victorious Thought Police – the Cadburyesque bar of chocolate which sets him thinking about a different quality of experience, the picture of St Clement's Dane, the idyllic rural landscapes in which the most dubiously 'romantic' parts of the book are set, and the fragments of popular culture: the nursery rhyme which no-one can quite remember and the surviving conviviality of the proles in the pub. Orwell's novel establishes these as physical or social *presences*, and distinguishes them from the archival material which the Party controls so thoroughly. These presences are for the good; they are valued as traces or residues of a more humane order of society. More than this, the novel suggests that they are capable of rehumanising people – that a person coming into contact with such traces can be reintegrated to an extent, with memories beginning to make sense again and externally repressed or uprooted feelings coming back to life.

History and the Inner City

Orwell situated his celebrated prole quarter somewhere north of a no longer existing Saint Pancras Station. While it is chaotic, deprived and dishevelled, the area is presented as being less vigorously policed and confined, a zone in which fundamental human values consequently survive. There is, of course, no point in searching out the literal reality of the prole quarter, but things nonetheless remain to be said about such inner city areas as they really are in the 1980s. I shall start somewhere north-east of the prole quarter in Stoke Newington. This has the convenience of being where I live, but it is also fairly representative of the many city areas in which a white working class coexists with a diversity of 'minority' groups and an incoming middle class.

An increasingly conscious *preservational* emphasis has established itself in this area over recent years – an emphasis which is more contemporary and extravagant than the one rather tired blue plaque which we have to mark the spot where Daniel Defoe once lived. This emphasis is closely connected with what is often called 'gentrification' – a process which has certainly taken place here between Orwell's time (when the area's Victorian terraced houses were scarcely marketable at all) and a present day rich in mortgages (for those who can afford them) and improvement grants, and in which the most caved-in old hovel is likely to fetch £30,000 as long as it has been emptied of sitting tenants. The houses which the planners of the 1960s were so eager to decry as slums are being refitted in more senses than one.

The middle classes have been moving in since the late Sixties at least. We bring with us, as everyone knows, a market for wine bars and the like, but we also come into the area with an attention of our own, with ways of understanding and 'appropriating' the place we have entered. So it happens that there is a market for those very 19th century fittings (cast iron fireplaces, sash windows) which the renovators were ripping out only a couple of years ago when *modernisation* was still the essence of conversion. So it happens that small voluntary associations with an interest in the area's architectural heritage spring up, producing booklets with titles like *The Victorian Villas of Hackney* and organising tours of the area. So it happens that the few enamelled signs – 'Win her affection with A1 Confections' – remaining above shop fronts or the barely visible traces of war-time camouflage paint on the town hall are brought into a new kind of focus by some passersby. So it happens that the classical junk shops of Orwell's prole quarter – shops in which a few ordinary but irreplaceable 'treasures' might be found among the general accumulation of undeniably local detritus – are being augmented by a new kind of 'not-quite-antique' shop in which the selection has already been made by well-travelled proprietors who value old things rather as Orwell himself did. So it also happens that this contemporary preservational emphasis comes to be linked with the development of official policy. Stoke Newington Church Street has recently been declared a preservation area, and the newly rediscovered grave of the great nineteenth century Chartist Bronterre O'Brien is to be restored (with the GLC's financial assistance) in the local cemetery.

In this new perspective Stoke Newington oscillates between its contemporary reality as part of the inner city and an imaginative reconstruction of its past as a dissenting community (which it was in Defoe's time) that even the plague, according to some accounts, never really entered. This imagined past keeps looming into view: 'That Spar shop over there ... it's really an eighteenth century hostelry. And underneath that greengrocer's next door there are cellars where the horses used to be stabled.' Traces remain, as one might say, except that this preservational attention is not automatically granted to residues which have survived neglect, decay and the barbarism of post-war planning. It has a more subjective side as well, involving as it does a contemporary *orientation* towards the past rather than just the survival of old things. There are indeed some fine 18th century town houses, the odd bow window and other such residues, but there is also an increased inclination to value the past, to notice and cherish it, to move into it and maintain it as a presence in our lives. To a considerable extent, I suggest, middle class incomers have brought with them Orwell's fond perspective on the prole quarter – a perspective which is not based on the cherishing of things and places that have been lived with for years, but which finds its basis in a more abstract 'aestheticisation' of the ordinary and the old.

Meanwhile, Stoke Newington has been administratively integrated into Hackney, a borough which earlier this year was declared to be the poorest in the United Kingdom. This suggests other perceptions of the place. There are clear indications of the ongoing and customary practices of a white working class community – indications which may well be resignified and mythologised within the incoming middle class perspective, but which are not in themselves mere hallucinations. However, if some of the cultural relations of this white working class have survived the upheavals of the post-war period, they do so within an encompassing sense of anxiety. It only took one person (an incomer) to walk into the local pub last Spring with a jug, and the intention of taking beer home, for conversation to pause before a torrent of memories started to flow:

'When I was a girl I used to fetch for my Grandad' and 'Of course that' 10s a four pint jug – what do you think it was made for?' Such discussion forms an act of commemoration in a full sense of that word – a sharing of memories, certainly, but also tribute and testimony to a valued time which is increasingly alienated from the present and only to be recalled occasionally. And there were indeed some for whom this sort of replay was uneasy – the younger people, by and large, who distinctly didn't join in and who may also have gone further, saying they wanted nothing to do with all that. A few weeks later during the election campaign, these same sceptics would sit at the bar scoffing at Michael Foot as the television showed him evading questions about defence and going on about the Forties and the traditions of the Labour Party. 'There he goes, Old Worzel ...'

A similar sense of upheaval was evident during the encounters-at-the-standpipe which were laid on for us during the water strike at the beginning of 1983. 'Just like the old days', as one woman remarked in the cold but almost convivial misery of a momentarily reactivated street corner, a remark which resounded with ambiguity, contra-diction of feeling and (once uttered) embarrassment – perhaps at the way deep feeling and cliché can run so cruelly together. As for the embitterment and reaction which grows in such a context, it will take me a few years to forget the somewhat dishevelled elderly man who happened to make his way down the pavement as we were moving in. 'People moving in', he said with affected surprise and a certain amount of contempt in his voice. 'People (by which he meant white people) still moving in.' He went on to comment that had he been able to he would have moved *out* years ago, along with the many he had known leave for the suburbs and new towns in the Fifties and Sixties.

While I do not wish to pass off these anecdotes in place of analysis, I do take them to indicate how much this traditional white working class has been affected by a dislocation of memory not entirely unlike that which Orwell describes in *Nineteen Eighty-Four*. And of course things *have* changed. Police helicopters hover overhead and shoppers find the High Street filled with often burly and even more often rude blue men and women engaged in community policing. There have been demonstrations (and mass arrests) and graffiti has been appearing on the walls: 'Police scum killed Colin Roach – We are getting angry' and 'Police pigs murdered Colin Roach'. Graffiti has also been disappearing, the large and loud letters sprayed along the length of Church Street quickly silenced by someone who followed the same route with brush and yellow paint – not a 'memory hole' exactly but another act, one suspects, of community policing.

It may be presumptuous, but I'll hazard a guess that the people who took up Colin Roach as cause and symbol aren't too concerned about old enamelled signs and Chartists, or the fact that Church Street has been declared a preservation area. For the large and mixed black population living in the Hackney/Stoke Newington area is still struggling against formidable odds for the basic constitutional and cultural rights of a citizenship which for many is not much more than formally secured. History from this point of view remains to be made; and the cultural rights to develop and assert a different past or, in wider terms, a different experience of the same history. From this point of view the other appropriations of the past which I have just described may well constitute part of the problem, in that they value a time *before* post-war immigration. And this, given how often British myths of history bear with them colonialist and racist ideas about 'subject peoples', is to stay at the more innocent end of the spectrum of racism. For if the 1970s brought the Habitat style of interior decor into this area, they also saw the rise of the National Front.

The National Past

So people live in different worlds even though they may share the same locality, and in this respect place is secondary to the social and political processes defining people and their inter-relations. The Colin Roach case indicated this very clearly. To many residents Colin Roach's death in the foyer of Stoke Newington police station was scarcely more 'local' than any other event in the media – something one heard about on the news. But this is not just a matter of distance between different people or groups – of relations which are merely absent or not yet made – for one can't make this point without also raising the larger question of domination and subordination: without, in other words, recognising that relations *do* exist even though they are not always directly experienced. For the worlds inhabited by some groups can work against the needs and interests of others, defining them according to an imported logic, romanticising and mythologising them, confining them to the margins of public life. While this process of cultural domination is often not consciously and intentionally motivated it occurs at both national and local levels; and a publicly instituted sense of history, tradition and national identity does indeed play a formidable and increasing part in it. How, then, is a sense of history – of past and identity – articulated into these wider political processes at the national level?

   First, it is worth recalling Orwell's portrayal of a past controlled directly and totally from above. It is clear that this sort of manipulation does go on, and not just in the Soviet bloc. States have always tended to legitimise themselves by structuring 'the past' into their own present order of appearance. And the process continues strongly enough in Britain today. To quote only one example, Keith Joseph, Secretary for Education, has recently refused a number of proposed syllabus systems for the teaching of history in schools, finding them insufficiently assiduous in their promotion of the mythical, rather than simply historical, values of national unity and pride.[2] Such manipulation from above may not always work in practice, but in attempting such a thing Joseph himself is acting in a genuinely traditional way. For it is a time-honoured national tradition in this country for aspects of history to be obliterated, for others to be rewritten, and for supposedly 'immemorial' traditions to be synthetically created to fill and command the void left as 'colonial' cultures and histories are anthropologised (made 'primitive'), rerouted or destroyed.[3]

But while such deliberate control of the past has a clear place in the picture, we are not only dealing with coercion from above. For a start, the complex sense of the national past which is established in public consciousness is the product of a whole combination of processes occurring over a far wider social territory than the books and schools that questions of 'history' are normally thought to occupy. It is, for example, central to the current prominence of the national past that the public, far from just being passive bearers of prescriptions from above, is strongly inclined in that direction. Often referred to as 'nostalgia', this testifies to a crisis in the way we think about the historical process itself – a crisis which has left the future unimaginable and, indeed, unachievable to a widening range of people.

This crisis doesn't come from nowhere. It reflects the continued economic decline of Britain and also the enormous transformation and destruction of customary and traditional social relations which have occurred in the post-war period. Communities have been destroyed by 'planned' development, certainly, but this period has also seen the dislocation of generally accepted ideas (about family life or work, for example), cultural patterns of behaviour and expectation, memory and a good deal more besides. As if this wasn't enough, the ideas of progress – of 'growth' or technological innovation – which underpinned the mixed economy of the post-war settlement have also collapsed, leaving us thankful for mere holding measures like North Sea oil or, on a different level, the various economic and social 'remedies' (from monetarism to 'Victorian values') to be found in the New Conservatism's Almanack. We are left, it often seems, with little confidence in the future and an anxious tendency to look back, cherishing what we see slipping away behind us and wondering what can reasonably be expected to come next on the uphill road to the abyss.

As we know, Margaret Thatcher has devised a politics which speaks to this orientation. She has offered a restoration of Victorian values as her cultural accompaniment to the restoration of Victorian Villas in some of our inner city areas. This is no purely new phenomenon, and throughout this century there have been reasons enough to look back and wonder. As should be clear to anyone aware of the anti-industrialism of the preservation movement, which finds its late 19th century roots in the endeavours of William Morris, Octavia Hill and others, or of the political utopia made out of 'Merrie England' by earlier English socialists like Blatchford and the Hammonds, this orientation towards the past is not the sole preserve of the Right. Even so, it is increasingly evident in such examples as the progressive traditionalism of Royal ceremony and display.[4]

Representations of the past are not static, however, even in the apparently dominant culture of Imperialism. A fairly light example of this can be found in the transformation of cricket, that 'quintessentially English' game which was taken in the name of civilisation to the colonies and came back as a game that 'colonials' had appropriated and won. Then came the myths of violation – of what was no longer 'cricket'. The Australians (especially since the 'vulgarity' of Kerry Packer) wear bright clothes and bowl with dangerous aggression. The West Indians come with audiences that don't just clap more often than once every eight seconds; they drum, smoke ganja, drink Special Brew, dance and storm the pitch. As one response to this development goes, if the West Indians now win then it must be because they bowl unfairly and bring the jungle into this land of greensward and topiary, setting up such a cacophony that gentlemen cricketers can't concentrate ...

As this last example suggests, it is no *simple* process of domination through which 'high culture' has achieved a more general and 'national' status. Whatever else has been going on, there has been a movement towards the democratisation of culture. The achievements of socialist and feminist historians, for example, have played a substantial part in writing subordinated and ignored sections of society back into the history of this nation. But things have also been happening outside the disciplined space of historiographical research and argument. Consequently the same process can be seen in the post-war expansion of the National Heritage. Not too long ago at all, the National Heritage was made up almost exclusively of stately homes, irreplaceable antiques, works of art and the like: it was defined, in other words, according to academic definitions of Beauty and Historical Significance. Since the war the National Heritage has been opened to accommodate the ordinary (craft skills, techniques, etc.), the local, the familiar and, as Ironbridge Gorge testifies, to the archaeology of early industrialism.

From the point of view of domination this expansion has helped to produce a mythical collectivity, a 'we' which is certainly not fully inclusive. This 'we' brings people together in a shared celebration of an imagined national past and identity, and in doing so it softens (without in any way solving) the political differences between those included. As for those who are not included, all too often the same processes that consolidate the 'we' define those outside as 'Other' – outsiders who are often portrayed as threats to the collectivity itself. Despite arguments to the contrary, it is here that you find clear links between the working of nationalism and racism.[5] From the other side, however, it has to be added that people have worked hard to win this expansion of the National Heritage, and its extension into new areas also marks an important attribution of national significance to precisely those cultures (regional, domestic, working class, to do with production) which were previously ignored.

And yet if such difference is comprised within it, what is it that allows the national past to work so coherently as a combination with general popular appeal? It seems to me that the major factor is to be found in the shared anxieties which direct people towards the past in the first place. The national past owes its profoundly utopian radiance and its unity to the fact that it bears the projected hopes for a better world and the displaced desire for gratifications not readily available in contemporary experience. But what really matters is how this heterodox combination is actually *mobilised* in contemporary political life.

The first three years of this decade have seen the national past played as a winning card in the hand of a New Conservatism concerned to legitimise an extreme monetarist policy. It is not just the Labour Party (tied so closely in the public mind to that grey 'national interest' that Harold Wilson and other leaders of post-war bureaucratic statist reform invoked so tirelessly) which has suffered by this new appeal to the nation. Since the Falklands it has also been lined up against the softer 'one-nation' Conservatism of such 'wets' as Gilmour, Pym and those champions of the National Heritage Act (1980), St John Stevas and Patrick Cormack.

The challenge facing those committed to the radicalisation of democracy – to Socialism in that sense – is to develop models for social development which, rather than fetishising an imagined past or feeding on public anxieties about the future, work to re-establish public confidence in history as a process that can still move forward for the better. This is a question, therefore, of re-establishing that a more Socialist *and* desirable future can indeed be made, not of establishing a sentimentalist view of the past which could be called Labour's own. Such a reinstatement will not be based on the exclusion and marginalisation of some members of British society. It will start where we are, not where we are inclined to think some of us have been.

And what of a place like Stoke Newington? The predominantly Labour-voting inner city areas are burdened enough with poverty and social aggravation, and the Conservative government is working – in the name of the 'nation' – quite deliberately to grind them even further down. But other possibilities are also visible. There is by now something resembling a tradition of community politics based in the inner cities of this country; and despite undoubted problems this has ramifications in terms of public involvement in the development (rather than the mere consumption) of social services. There is also cultural activity of an exemplary kind. As I have said, Stoke Newington is part of Hackney, and a number of years ago the People's Autobiography of Hackney began to produce a series of books based on local people's (often tape recorded) memories, collectively discussed, and reproduced largely in their own words. Not only did these open up history in a totally new light – street corner stories, working experiences – as opposed to the flow of supposedly 'major' events – they started a pattern of similar projects around the country in which working class history has been captured and 'broadcast'. Developments such as these, indicating as they do a different consciousness of history firmly attached to issues and initiatives in the *present*, justify the admittedly optimistic thought that perhaps it will be in these very areas that such a future first comes into practical definition. And no matter how quietly, we would then be talking about making history in a very different sense.

Authors

Crispin Aubrey is a freelance journalist and writer, and the author of *Who's Watching You?* – a book about some of the realities of state surveillance in the 1970s.

Paul Chilton teaches linguistics and literature in the Department of French Studies at the University of Warwick. He has previously written on the subject of nuclear language – Nukespeak.

Mike Cooley and **Mike Johnson** both work in the technology division of the Greater London Enterprise Board. Their work connects a critical approach to modern technology with practical initiatives – assisting human control over technology and production rather than the other way round. The newly established Technology Network provides a possible framework for these objectives.

Philip Corrigan was temporary lecturer, Institute of Education, University of London; he is now professor, Department of Sociology, OISE, University of Toronto, Canada.

Paul Lashmar has spent the last 5 years with the *Observer* and is an investigative journalist.

Florence Lewis is an English teacher in the United States.

Peter Moss Peter is in the Education Department, University of Adelaide, Australia. He coedits *Category B*, an alternative teachers' magazine. He has written *Sounds Real* and several articles on the media.

Christopher Roper is, after 12 years of publishing a newsletter on Latin America, now looking at how computers are changing the ways in which information is transferred.

Jenny Taylor is a lecturer in Literature at Bradford University. She is the editor of *Notebooks/Memoirs/ARchives: Reading and Re-reading, Doris Lessing* and is currently writing a book about the Sensation Novel of the 1980s.

Colin Ward's books include *Anarchy in Action, Tenants Take Over* and *The Child in the City*.

David Widgery's next book, a study of music, sex and politics called *Beating Time* is published by Writers and Readers in 1985 and he has on the stocks a sequel to his Penguin *The Left in Britain 1956–68*.

Patrick Wright was born in 1951, year of the Festival of Britain and has been reeling ever since.

Notes

Introduction

1. Quoted by Bernard Crick, *George Orwell. A Life* (Secker and Warburg) 1981, p.395. Orwell was perhaps optimistic (for once) in representing this state of affairs as leading to a kind of permanently stable state of mutual deterrence ...
2. George Kateb, 'The Road to *1984*' in S. Hynes (ed.), *Twentieth Century Interpretations of 1984* (Prentice Hall) 1971.

Chapter 3: Desire is Thoughtcrime

1. George Orwell: *The Road to Wigan Pier* (Penguin, 1962) pp.104–5.
2. George Orwell: *Nineteen Eighty-Four* (Penguin, 1954) pp. 20–1.
3. *The Road to Wigan Pier*, p. 15.
4. *Nineteen Eighty-Four*, p. 52.
5. For a more detailed analysis of this, see Elizabeth Wilson: *Only Halfway to Paradise: Women in Post-War Britain: 1945–1968* (Tavistock, 1980).
6. *Nineteen Eighty-Four*, pp. 56–8.
7. As above, p. 109.
8. As above, p. 59.
9. As above, p. 16.
10. As above, p. 28.
11. As above, p. 104.
12. Raymond Williams: *Orwell* (Fontana, 1971) p. 81.
13. George Orwell, 'Inside the Whale', reprinted in *The Collected Essays, Journalism and Letters, Volume I, 1920–1940* (Harmondsworth, Penguin, 1979) p 548.
14. A more elaborate critique of the notion of sexual repression and account of the historical construction of sexuality can be found in Michel Foucault, *The History of Sexuality, Volume One, An Introduction* (London, Allen Lane, 1979) and Jeffrey Weeks, *Sex, Politics and Society* (London, Longman, 1981).
15. All definitions are taken from *The Oxford English Dictionary*.

Chapter 4: Newspeak: It's The Real Thing

1. Basil Bernstein: *Class, Codes and Control* (Routledge and Kegan Paul, 1971).
2. Bob Hodge and Roger Fowler: 'Orwellian Linguistics' in Fowler, R. et al. (eds.) *Language and Control* (Routledge and Kegan Paul, 1979).
3. Murray Edelman: *Political Language: Words that Succeed and Policies that Fail* (New York, Academic Press, 1977) chapter 6.
4. See for instance Labov, W.: 'The Logic of Non-standard English' in Giglioli, P. (ed.) *Language and Social Context* (Penguin, 1972).
5. Edelman, p. 109, as above.
6. Claire Lerman: 'Dominant Discourse: the Institutional Voice and Control of Topic' in Davis, H. and Walton, P. *Language, Image, Media* (Blackwell, 1983).
7. *Nineteen Eighty-Four* (Penguin, 1962) pp. 44–5.
8. Another common metaphor for unemployment is that of disease: 'the cancer of

unemployment', for instance. The noun unemployment may also be revealing. Both employment and unemployment act as abstract nouns, and obscure the fact that what is referred to is not a thing, but a process and an economic relationship. Note also that while *employment can* refer to a process (A employs B), *unemployment* can not (A unemploys B ??).

9. Quoted by Lerman, p. 99, as above.
10. *Nineteen Eighty-Four*, p. 161.
11. See Paul Chilton: 'War, Work and Falk Talk' in *Category B*, No. 4, March 1983 (Alternative English Co-operative, Magill, South Australia) pp. 17–26.
12. *The Road to Wigan Pier* (Penguin, 1970) pp. 43–4.

Chapter 5: The Tyranny of Language

1. Peter Funt: 'TV news: seeing isn't believing' (*Saturday Review*, Nov. 7, 1980).
2. Project Censored was the idea of Professor Carl Jensen, Media Studies department, Sonoma State University, Rohnert Park, California 94928.
3. Anita R. Schiller and Herbert I. Schiller: 'Who Can Own What America Knows' (*The Nation*, April 17, 1982).
4. *Nineteen Eighty-Four* (Penguin, 1967) p. 247.
5. See Stephen Hilgartner et al.: *Nukespeak* (Penguin, New York, 1983).
6. *Newsweek* (June 13, 1983).
7. As above.
8. See a column on business by economist Milton Friedman (*Newsweek*, June 13, 1983) which has FHLBB (Federal Home Loan Bank Board), PLAM (Price Level Adjusted Mortgage), PLAD (Price Level Adjusted Deposit), CPI (Calculated Price Index) and S & L (Savings and Loan).
9. See Richard A. Blake: 'The Attraction of the Moonies' (*America*, Feb. 1980) p. 83.
10. Shirley Hazard: 'We Need Silence to Find Out What We Think (*The New York Times Book Review*, Nov. 14, 1952) p. 28.
11. *The Guardian* (Jan. 5, 1983).
12. McCabe contributed numerous pieces to *The San Francisco Chronicle* between 1966 and 1974.
13. *The New York Times* (May 9, 1974).
14. *The New Yorker* (December, 1982).

Chapter 7: The Robots' Return?

1. From an interview with Weitzenbaum, 'The Man in the Belly of the Beast' (*The Observer*, Aug. 18, 1982).
2. *Nineteen Eighty-Four*, p. 154.
3. *American Machinist*, July, 1979.
4. Karl Marx: *Capital* Vol. I, p. 508 (Penguin edition).
5. As note 1.
6. A. Sanberg: *Computer Dividing Man and Work* (Arbetslivcentrum, Stockholm, 1979) p. 81.
7. *Work Study* No. 23, 1974, pp. 23–9.
8. Mike Cooley: *Architect or Bee: The Human/Technology Relationship* (Langley Technical Services, 1980).

Chapter 8: Information as Power

1. Final Report, *Foreign and Military Intelligence* (United States Select Committee

to study Governmental Operations with respect to Intelligence Activities, April 26, 1976).

2. Ackroyd, Margolis, Rosenhead and Shallice: *The Technology of Political Control* (Penguin, 1977).
3. See Duncan Campbell: *War Plan UK* (Burnett Books, 1982).
4. Final Report, *Working Party into Community/Police Relations in Lambeth* (Jan. 1981).
5. See Jonathan Bloch and Pat Fitzgerald: *British Intelligence and Covert Action* (Junction Books, 1983).
6. Peter Taylor: *Beating the Terrorists* (Penguin, 1980).
7. See Celina Bledowski (ed.): *War and Order* (Junction Books, 1983).
8. *The Interception of Communications in Great Britain* (HMSO, Cmnd 7873, 1980).
9. See *New Statesman*, Feb. 15, 1980.
10. Duncan Campbell: *Phonetappers and the Security State* (New Statesman Report No. 2).
11. As above.
12. *State Research Bulletin* No. 3 (Dec. 1977).
13. 'Taxman sets trap for Jet-set exile' (*The Observer*, May 22, 1983).
14. See *The Police Use of Computers* (Technical Authors Group, Occasional Publication No. 1) and Peter Hain (ed.): *Policing the Police* (John Calder, 1980).
15. Roger Cross: 'Police Computers on Trial' (*Yorkshire Post*, June 10, 1983).
16. Ray Rodgers: 'The Computer Detective' (*The Observer*, July 10, 1983).
17. *State Research Bulletin* No. 13 (Aug. 1979).
18. David Leigh: 'Police Give Computer Secrets Out' (*The Observer*, Oct. 4, 1981).
19. Figure from *Policing The Police*, see, note 14.
20. David Leigh: 'Alderson Scraps Files of Special Branch' (*The Observer*, Jan. 10, 1982).
21. David Leigh: 'Special Branch's dossier on SDP member revealed' (*The Observer*, Jan. 31, 1982).
22. NCCL Annual Report, 1982.
23. See *Policing The Police*, note 14.
24. *National Times*, May 20–26, 1983.
25. *Freedom and the Security Services* (Labour Party, 1983).

Chapter 9: Big Brother Drives a Bulldozer

1. Derek Fraser and Anthony Sutcliffe: Introduction to Fraser and Sutcliffe (eds.): *The Pursuit of Urban History* (Edward Arnold, 1983).
2. Norman Dennis: *People and Planning* (Faber, 1970).
3. Bruce Allsop: *Towards a Humane Architecture* (Frederick Muller, 1974).
4. T. Dan Smith: *An Autobiography* (Oriel Press, 1970).
5. Wilfred Burns: *New Towns for Old* (Leonard Hill, 1963).
6. As above.
7. Alison Ravetz: *Remaking Cities* (Croom Helm, 1980).
8. Andrew Gibb: *Glasgow: The Making of a City* (Croom Helm, 1983).
9. Jon Gower Davies: *The Evangelistic Bureaucrat* (Tavistock, 1972).
10. J. I. Gershuny and R. E. Pahl: 'Britain in the decade of the three economies' (*New Society* Jan. 3, 1980).
11. R. E. Pahl: 'Employment, work and the domestic division of labour' in Michael Harloe and Elizabeth Lebas (eds.): *City, Class and Capital* (Edward Arnold, 1981).

Chapter 10:   Hard Machines, Soft Messages

1. According to Orwell's *Collected Essays* (Penguin, 1970, Volume 4) he began publishing articles around 1928 and his first book was published in 1933. All future references to this volume will be in the form *CE4*; references to *1984* are to the Penguin edition, reprinted in 1968.

2. I disagree with other contributors in finding value in the *first* part of Anthony Burgess' *1985* (Arrow, 1980), especially '1948: an old man interviewed' (pp. 20–39) which stresses the 1948 in *1984*. In Orwell's novel notice the discussion of shortages (e.g. p. 42); bombing (pp. 70–71, p. 122); and the use of message forms with standard phrases (p. 91), a form of communication imposed on service personnel for telegrams to relations in Britain. Orwell wrote to Richard Rees on March 16, 1949: 'Have you torn up your clothing book? (Clothes rationing ended on Feb. 1, 1949). The reaction of everybody here was the same – "it must be a trap". Of course clothes are now sufficiently rationed by price. I think I shall order myself a new jacket all the same.' (*CE4*, p. 544). A good survey of rationing is Angus Calder's *People's War* (Panther, 1971).

3. Burgess report (*1985*, p. 21) that the Italian edition of *1984* mistranslates this to have the clocks striking one!

4. This has been a major theme in the work of Jeremy Seabrook, for example in his book *What Went Wrong?* (Gollancz, 1978) and his articles in *The Guardian* in 1982.

5. One excellent local study is *Brighton on the Rocks: Monetarism and the Local State* (Queenspark, 1983).

6. See the reports in *The Sunday Times* and *The Observer* July 3, 1983.

7. Vance Packard was the first to alert me to the confusion between 'The Good Life' (a moral-politicpal category) and the possession of goods (consumption and spectacle). In fact 'that' signal was one which was being beamed from inside that Great Society of abundance (the USA) for those who wanted to watch for it. In the long tradition of cultural criticism (Film-noir, detective fiction, melodrama, musicals) the mid-1950s registered the life that could not speak its name in the USA. The poems of the 'Beat Generation' (1956) for example, or his poem *America* (1956); and consider the following in terms of the themes of *1984*:

   'Williams says it over and over. Chris Maclaine once smeared it across a full page of his magazine and had copies returned – as he might have expected – from all the bookstores, in terror: THE AMERICAN PEOPLE ARE AFRAID. Of our country, and ourselves in it. Why not? A dark and bloody ground. Vast, terrifying, all of it a precipice. How to live in it, L I V E in it: not hide, run, die, every way but biologically. That too even.'

   'The fear and violence remain. In this country the best talk only in fragments and whispers ...'

   Frederick Eckman: 'Toccata and Fuge' (*Odyssey*, 2(1) December *1959*).

8 I am thinking here of the material collected in R. Vaneigem: *Revolution of Everyday Life* (orig. 1967) English ed., Rising Free Collective, 1979; G. Debord: *The Society of the Spectacle* (orig. 1967) English ed., B. M. Mattoid, 1972; and the excellent collection *Situationist International Anthology* (Berkeley, Calif., Bureau of Public Secrets, 1981). A more 'theoretical' (and in my view less progressive) treatment can be traced in the work of Jean Baudrillard: *The Mirror of Production* (Telos Press, 1975) and *For a Critique of the Political Economy of the Sign* (Telos Press, 1981).

Chapter 11:   The Conscription of History

1   Soviet Communism has certainly excelled itself in obliterating archives and a great deal more besides. This point can be made briefly enough by quoting a story told in F. Feher, A. Heller & G. Markus: *Dictatorship Over Needs* (Blackwell, 1983): 'In a meeting with young people seven years ago, Yevtushenko made an improvised survey regarding their estimation of the number of Stalin's victims: he was told that there had probably been as many as thousands.' (p. 152). The real number, of course, went far into the millions.

2.   See Martin Walker: 'Tory Historians Find a Heritage to Nationalise' (*The Guardian*, June 6, 1983).

3.   See E. Hobsbawm and T. Ranger (eds.): *The Invention of Tradition* (Cambridge University Press, 1983), particularly Bernard S. Cohn's 'Representing Authority in Victorian India' and T. Ranger's 'The Invention of Tradition in Colonial Africa'.

4.   See David Cannadine's essay 'The Context, Performance and Meaning of Ritual; the British Monarchy and the "Invention of Tradition" in the same book as the two essays mentioned above.

5.   See Benedict Anderson: *Imagined Communities; Reflections on the Origin and Spread of Nationalism* 1 (Verso, 1983), particularly the chapter on 'Patriotism and Racism' (pp. 129–140).

BILL EVANS

Comedia Publishing Group
9 Poland St, London W1

Comedia Publishing produces books on all aspects of the media including: the press and publishing; TV, radio and film; and the impact of new communications technology.

The Comedia publishing series is based on contemporary research of relevance to media and communications studies courses, though it is also aimed at general readers, activists and specialists in the field.

The series is exceptional because it spans the media from the mainstream and commercial to the oppositional, radical and ephemeral.

No. 19 **COMMUNITY, ART & THE STATE: A different prescription** by Owen Kelly.

In this book Owen Kelly takes a polemical view of the way that community art has developed in this country, the way that development has been guided by the types of funding it has received, and the way in which it has often served the interests of the state, and the status quo, which it was allegedly seeing to change. He establishes the outlines of a different strategy: one which would build upon the strengths of community art, but avoid the danger that community artists currently face – of being licensed rebels whose very licence makes them ineffectual. Owen Kelly has been working as a community artist in South London for seven years, and has chaired the Greater London Arts Association's Community Arts Panel.

paperback £2.95 hardback £9.50

No. 18 **PRESS, RADIO & TELEVISION — An introduction** by Comedia

This large format pamphlet is produced in cooperation with the Workers Educational Association. It includes outlines of the basic structures of the newspaper industry, television and radio broadcasting in this country, critical introductions to the study of their output, and points to the key issues facing these media in the future.

paperback only £1.50

No. 17 **NINETEEN EIGHTY-FOUR IN 1984: Autonomy, Control & Communication**

edited by Paul Chilton and Crispin Aubrey

Nineteen Eighty-Four has entered English culture as a by-word for a wired-up world of alienation and surveillance. The revolution in communications technology is often seen as synonymous with creeping growth of state oppression. It is the capitalist democracies which have created the information revolution, but will that technology lead us down a totalitarian path? The book examines to what extent the picture painted by Orwell provides an accurate reflection of 1984 as it is, and looks at developments in the control of work, leisure and the environment and the role played by

censorship, propaganda, intelligence and surveillance.
paperback £3.95 hardback £10.50

No. 16 **TELEVISING 'TERRORISM': Political violence in popular culture**
Philip Schlesinger, Graham Murdock and Philip Elliott
Television has often been accused of promoting the cause of
terrorist violence. In this unusual book – one which is full of telling
illustrations – the authors make a major contribution to the debate
on this question. Unlike other writers, they examine in detail a
range of television's output to see how the various perspectives on
terrorism are presented. A novel feature of the authors' approach is
the way they analyse not only factual coverage but also fictional
representations and the ways in which these relate to one another.
After discussing the work of critics both on the Right and the Left
they argue for a more sophisticated understanding of the way in
which television works.
paperback £4.95 hardback £12.00

No. 15 **CAPITAL: Local Radio & Private Profit**
Who benefits from commercial local radio: the public or the
shareholders? In this report Local Radio Workshop looks at the
relationship between profit and programming by focussing on
London's lucrative pop station, Capital Radio. They analyse the
origins of commercial local radio and Capital's history, programming and public relations, and show how, over the years,
Capital has pioneered a narrow form of 'local' broadcasting tuned
to the interests of advertisers and shareholders. Local Radio
Workshop argues that a reassessment of the role of private finance
in local radio is long overdue and makes proposals for achieving
greater public control of and participation in this important public
resource.
paperback £3.95 hardback £10.50

No. 14 **NOTHING LOCAL ABOUT IT: London's local radio**
by Local Radio Workshop
The report is based on an analysis of the materials broadcast in one
week by London's three 'local' stations: Capital, LBC and BBC
Radio London. It was written by LRW, Black Women's Radio
Group, Women's Airwaves and Rest of the News with special
contributions from SWAPO and the London Business School etc.
In addition the new edition contains a selection of responses to the
original report.
paperback £3.95 hardback £10.50

No. 13 **MICROCHIPS WITH EVERYTHING — The consequences of
information technology**
edited by Paul Sieghar
Information Technology is the result of the rapid advance of telecommunications and computing technologies. Books on the
subject so far have been confined to either specialist areas or the
needs of the computer buff; this book recognises that IT affects

every aspect of our lives – the political, social and cultural. Alan Benjamin, Clive Jenkins, Mike Cooley, Patricia Hewitt and Stuart Hood.
paperback £3.50 hardback £9.50
Published jointly with the Institute of Contemporary Arts

No. 12 **THE WORLD WIRED UP — Unscrambling the new communication s puzzle**
by Brian Murphy
Will the new computer-communications systems really create the social revolution in work and leisure they promise? This book attempts to puncture the hot air balloon on which the industry currently rides by firstly cutting through the jargon to describe the new systems – especially satellite broadcasting, cable television and 'informatics' – and then explaining how the world market is being carved up by the multinationals. Brian Murphy's lucid text sorts out the main players and their products and also examines the options for control available to governments and citizens.
paperback £3.50 hardback £9.50

No. 11 **WHAT'S THIS CHANNEL FOUR? — An Alternative report**
edited by Simon Blanchard and David Morley
Arguments about what sort of service a Fourth TV Channel should provide go back more than 20 years. But now it has finally become a reality, alongside its Welsh counterpart. Will Channel 4 live up to the expectations of innovation and experimentation – not simply providing an ITV2? This handbook explains how a major new broadcasting service was created, how it works from the inside, analyses the arguments about what programmes it will produce and shows how viewers can influence the content.
paperback £3.50 hardback £9.50

No. 10 **IT AIN'T HALF RACIST, MUM — Fighting racism in the media**
edited by Phil Cohen
A comprehensive analysis of racist attitudes and practices in the media, including interviews with black journalists and broadcasters. Articles range from an examination of positive discrimination policies at the new Channel Four to a critical look at how TV handles race in documentaries and drama programmes to an assessment of British media coverage of South Africa. Also outlined are specific campaigning activities against black under-employment and biased reporting.
paperback £2.50 hardback £7.50
Jointly published by Comedia and the Campaign Against Racism in the Media.

No. 9 **NUKESPEAK — The media and the bomb**
edited by Crispin Aubrey
paperback £2.50 hardback £7.50

No. 8   **NOT the BBC/IBA — The case for community radio**
by Simon Partridge
paperback £1.95 hardback £5.00

No. 7   **CHANGING THE WORD — The printing industry in transition**
by Alan Marshall
paperback £3.50 hardback £9.50

No. 6   **THE REPUBLIC OF LETTERS — Working class writing and local publishing**
edited by Dave Morley and Ken Worpole
paperback £3.95 hardback £8.50

No. 5   **NEWS LTD — Why you can't read all about it**
by Brian Whitaker
paperback £3.25 hardback £9.50

No. 4   **ROLLING OUR OWN — Women as printers, publishers and distributors**
by Eileen Cadman, Gail Chester, Agnes Pivot
paperback £2.25 hardback £7.50

No. 3   **THE OTHER SECRET SERVICE — Press distribution and press censorship**
by Liz Cooper, Charles Landry, Dave Berry
paperback only £0.80

No. 2   **WHERE IS THE OTHER NEWS — The news trade and the radical press**
by Dave Berry, Liz Cooper, Charles Landry
paperback £1.75 hardback £4.50

No. 1   **HERE IS THE OTHER NEWS — Challenges to the local commercial press**
by Crispin Aubrey, Charles Landry, Dave Morley
paperback £1.75 hardback £3.50